The Self-Awareness Workbook for Social Workers

The Self-Awareness Workbook for Social Workers

Juliet C. Rothman
The Catholic University of America

Allyn and Bacon
Boston • London • Toronto • Sydney • Tokyo • Singapore

Series Editor, Social Work and Family Therapy: Judy Fifer
Editor-in-Chief, Social Sciences: Karen Hanson
Editorial Assistant: Jennifer Muroff
Marketing Manager: Susan E. Ogar
Editorial–Production Service: Shepherd, Inc.
Composition and Prepress Buyer: Linda Cox
Manufacturing Buyer: Megan Cochran
Cover Administrator: Jenny Hart
Electronic Composition: Shepherd, Inc.

Copyright © 1999 by Allyn & Bacon
A Viacom Company
160 Gould Street
Needham Heights, MA 02494

Internet: www.abacon.com

Library of Congress Cataloging-in-Publication Data

Rothman, Juliet Cassuto
    The self-awareness workbook for social workers / Juliet C.
Rothman.
        p.   cm.
    Includes bibliographical references (p.   ) and index.
    ISBN 0-205-29029-9
    1. Social service—Vocational guidance.   2. Social workers—
    Psychology.   3. Self-perception.   I. Title.
HV40.R6844   1998
    361.3'023—dc21   98-21919
                                                                  CIP

Printed in the United States of America

10   9   8   7   6   5   4   3   03   02   01   00

In memory of my beloved son
Daniel,
who had chosen to dedicate his life
to the service of others

Contents

A Word to Instructors

This workbook has been designed to address the affective learning—the self-awareness—so necessary to effective and professional social work practice. There are three goals: (1) the development of an understanding of the value base of the profession and areas of difference and congruence between students' personal values and those of the profession; (2) growth in self-awareness in terms of the impact of life experiences and beliefs on the student's perception of those different from her- or himself; and (3) the exploration of a model for change which, through several immersion exercises, helps the student gain a deeper understanding of other groups.

There are three units in the workbook, each designed to focus primarily on one of the previously stated goals. Thus, Unit I explores the profession's value base and the student's motivation for selecting social work as a career. Unit II engages the student in a life review process of experiencing difference, both through personal experiences and in interaction with others. Unit III presents a model for change that asks the student to select a population, explore and experience with members of the population, and reassess beliefs and attitudes. Unit III also teaches this model for change so that the student may apply it throughout the course of her or his career to any group desired.

Units are composed of several chapters, each of which includes exercises that encourage the student to reflect on experiences, beliefs, and attitudes. Because of the personal nature of these assignments, the workbook has been designed with tear-out pages for privacy, should this be desired. The workbook as a whole or any portions may be placed in a separate looseleaf binder.

In order to enable accountability and provide a basis for grading, each unit also concludes with a unit assignment that is less personal in nature, allowing the instructor to assess and evaluate the student's progress through the workbook. It is suggested that each assignment be three to five pages in length.

The workbook has been designed to maximize flexibility in usage, so that it may be used appropriately in a variety of courses and with many different teaching formats and styles. It may be interwoven with other course content, or it may be used as a separate learning experience. Material and assignments may serve as a basis or focus for classroom discussion if desired but may also be used independently by students.

Preface

You have chosen to join a very special profession. Social work has a long and distinguished tradition of dedication to humanitarian ideals. We are advocates, reformers, and providers of direct services. Always, we are concerned with the maximization of human potential for each of our clients and for all members of society.

Our professional milieu is varied and diverse. We work in social agencies, schools, hospitals, businesses, public agencies, nursing homes, and many other places. Our clients come to us from different races, religions, ethnic and culture groups, age groups, and other affiliations. They may belong to one or more minority groups in our society. They may look different, act differently, and think differently, both from each other and from us. As clients, however, they share one common feature: They have come to us for help; they are in need of service.

Assisting clients to reach their personal goals and to grow and change in ways that are meaningful to them requires that we understand the important role that their life experiences have played in their understanding of the world. Throughout the social work educational curriculum, the importance of understanding our clients both as unique individuals and as members of groups is a recurrent theme in learning to be of service to them.

Providing the help that clients need is, in part, a matter of motivation and intention on the part of the social worker. Providing *professional* help to clients from many different ethnic, racial, religious, and cultural groups, however, requires three vital things beyond this: a knowledge base, professional practice skills, and self-awareness.

An excellent population knowledge base may be obtained through the study of the major ethnic, religious, and social groups that are a part of our society. These include Latinos and Hispanics, such as Mexicans, Puerto Ricans, and Cubans, some of whom may be political refugees, others of whom may be illegal immigrants; African Americans, whose ancestors may have entered the United States freely or against their will as slaves; Asians, such as Chinese, Koreans, and the Japanese, who suffered internment during World War II; Native Americans, such as Navajo, Apache, and Eskimo, who may have had their tribal lands and culture forcibly taken from them, and whose way of life has been devalued and suppressed; women, a minority by reason of oppression, not numbers; gays and lesbians, whose civil rights may be severely compromised in certain areas; eastern European populations, such as refugees from the former Soviet Union; and many others. Each group, from Muslim to Philipino to lesbian to disabled, has its own "story." Textbooks, such as Hraba's *American Ethnicity,* will provide excellent information regarding many populations in our society, including immigration history, experiences in the United States, special ethnic characteristics, and current status.

Studies of populations in schools of social work are often area-specific. They tend to focus on the groups that are a strong presence in the local area: Mexicans in Los Angeles, Puerto Ricans in New York, African Americans in Washington, D.C., Chinese in San Francisco. If you are attending a school far from your home, you may encounter populations with which you are unfamiliar, and acquiring the necessary knowledge base will require extra attention from you.

The second basic element, professional practice skills, includes skills in interviewing in a manner sensitive to differences—one that includes an awareness of client values, worldview, affect, and demeanor—and an understanding of goals and priorities that may be culturally based. For example, a worker with ethnically sensitive practice skills would be aware of the importance of setting goals and developing interventions that are congruous with the client's worldview and belief system. Goals that tend toward empowerment and self-actualization, for example, may be inappropriate for clients from cultures where self-effacement is valued and where the good of the family and community is placed before the individual's good.

Developing skills as a culturally aware professional is essential to practice. Such texts as *Ethnic-Sensitive Social Work Practice* (W. Devore & E. Schlesinger, Fifth Edition, Allyn & Bacon, 1999) provide a practice-focused approach to addressing multicultural issues in social work.

The third element, personal exploration and self-awareness in relation to issues of individual and group identity, is also essential to culturally sensitive practice, and will be the focus of your studies in this workbook.

We do not enter the social work profession with a *tabula rasa* (blank slate). We enter the field with our own perspective, colored by our genetic inheritance, life experiences, and chosen and ascribed affiliations. We enter as individuals and also as members of many, often overlapping, groups.

Our personal milieu, the world in which we grew up and in which we now live, has had a strong impact on our understanding of ourselves and others, especially in terms of similarity and difference. It has given us certain views, attitudes, biases, stereotypes, and prejudices. We may be aware of some and unaware of others. Only one thing is certain: We *all* hold impressions—some positive, some negative—about our own group and about other groups.

Because the views we hold strongly affect our professional work with clients, it is important to bring our personal views into our conscious awareness. We may wish to try to change some of them; we may continue to hold others. We will not be able to eliminate all biases and negative impressions. They are often the products of a lifetime of learning and are difficult to eradicate. The goal here is *awareness:* awareness that will assist us in working with others, not a complete restructuring of worldview.

The exercises at the end of each chapter are meant to remain completely private should you so desire. It is recognized that the material you are being asked to explore and record is personal and sensitive. Thus, this workbook is yours alone, your private record of your journey toward cultural self-awareness. You may choose to separate the pages that you write from the workbook: all pages on which you are asked to write may be easily removed from the workbook to ensure privacy.

With increased awareness, you will find within yourself an increased openness to other ways of thinking and a greater insight into other kinds of life experiences. The model that will be used in Unit III will help you use this new openness in expanding your ability to understand and relate to groups you identify as different in some manner from your own.

The chapters in this workbook will ask that you explore areas that may be difficult and painful for you. You may find yourself avoiding the exercises at the end of each chapter. This is a natural reaction; confronting these issues carries a strong emotional overlay. You may find it helpful to form a discussion group with other members of your class to work through some of the issues that this study raises for you. You may wish to attempt to discuss them with family or friends as well. The discussion questions at the end of each chapter are a suggested guide for such conversations.

Each unit also has a written assignment that is used by your instructor to acknowledge the work that you are doing. While the contents of the workbook are private and personal, and may be shared only at your discretion, the assignments validate your work and demonstrate that you are able to apply the concepts you have learned.

Unit I begins with an exploration of the mission, goals, and value base of the profession. We will then move on to develop an understanding of your personal motivation for entering the field of social work. By considering and comparing these two perspectives—the professional and the personal—you will be able to explore points of convergence and divergence between you as a person and the social work profession.

Unit II builds a picture of the complex and multifaceted person that you are through an exploration of identity and identity development. As you are guided through the process of defining your own identity, you will also be learning about the various elements and influences that help to form an individual identity. This unit also includes an exploration of theories of identity development.

Unit III presents a model for exploration and possible change in perceptions you hold about a particular population that you select. You will be interacting with the population through reading, socializing, and participating in an activity. You may select your population through personal reflection, or select a population with whom you are working or would like to work. The population should not be one of which you are a member; that is another project altogether—also an interesting one!

Acknowledgments

I would like to thank my colleagues, whose interest, support, and encouragement have made this project possible. Elizabeth Plionis and Christine Anlauf Sabatino encouraged me to explore the creative integration of cross-cultural counseling material in theory and practice classes and worked jointly with me to develop the "Personal Values and Worldview" assignment. Suzanne Heurtin-Roberts assisted me in classroom testing the "Model for Change" in the diversity and societal oppression course, and Michele Hawkins stressed the necessity of self-awareness in the development of social welfare policy and programs.

I would also like to express my appreciation for the energy and enthusiasm my students have given to the exploration of the self-awareness issues addressed in this workbook. Not only were they open to exploration and to sharing with each other their work in self-awareness, but their efforts far above and beyond the requirements of the "Model for Change" assignment encouraged and inspired this endeavor.

Thanks are also due to the colleagues who reviewed this proposal and manuscript: Wynne DuBray, California State University–Sacramento; Walter Pierce, Barry University; Katherine van Wormer, University of Northern Iowa; Francisco A. Villarruel, Michigan State University; Gary L. Villereal, Arizona State University; and David Worster, University of New Hampshire.

Unit I

You and the Social Work Profession

The first unit of your workbook places a framework around the work that we will be doing. This framework will guide and support you and will give you a rationale and a context within which to explore self-awareness.

The framework has two separate, but interlocking, levels. The outer one is formed by the profession of social work. It is composed of the mission and goals of the profession and includes a special commitment to the traditional populations the profession serves: oppressed, at-risk, disempowered, poor, and vulnerable populations.

This outer framework rests upon the society within which you, the profession, and all of the populations served are contained.

The inner framework is personal. It is formed by the person that you are: the unique combination of values, goals, life experiences, and professional aspirations that you bring with you as you enter the social work profession. Your personal framework defines you. It also guides you in the choices that you make and the work that you do. It is through this personal framework that you have chosen to become a social worker.

We will explore both frameworks; in addition, we will reflect upon the points at which the outer and inner framework, the professional and the personal, merge. Those points will support and validate the professional choice you have made. However, there is never a complete parallel between person and profession, if for no other reason than that professional mission, values, and goals are very abstract, while your values and goals are grounded in personal experience. Therefore, we will also explore the points at which they diverge and consider the possible effects of such divergence.

Chapter 1 will present the profession's special commitment from a historical and ethical perspective. In Chapter 2, you will explore your own goals and values as related to the professional choice you have made. Chapter 3 will briefly explore the client–worker relationship in order to understand the impact on both client and worker of the imbalances inherent in the helping relationship. Chapter 4 will explore some of the characteristics of oppressed populations in the United States today.

Chapter ONE

A Very Special Mission

CÓS
+
Settlement Houses

The social work profession as we know it today has evolved through the combination of two equally important movements for societal change: the charity organization society and the settlement houses. Practitioners within each tradition recognized that, while methodologies and interventions might differ, they shared a common interest in, and strong commitment to, the same population. This population included all groups who were vulnerable, oppressed, and helpless in the face of overwhelming personal and institutional difficulties that impeded their human search for dignity, meaningfulness, self-respect, and personal fulfillment.

This commitment has been the focus, as well as one of the unique distinguishing characteristics, by which the profession has been defined, and it is this commitment that distinguishes social work from the other helping professions. The commitment involves direct intervention, advocacy, and policy formulation and planning, and it spans the broad continuum between micro and macro levels of practice.

A brief review of social work's historical perspective and of the tenets of the National Association of Social Workers (NASW) Code of Ethics will help to illustrate these historical roots and the current manifestations of this special commitment.

Historical Perspective

The Charitable Organization Societies

During the aftermath of the Civil War, the diverse needs of those severely affected by the war, such as newly freed slaves, soldiers, families, children, and residents of war-torn or destroyed areas, overwhelmed any existing charitable systems. The earliest social welfare agencies, the Children's Aid and Charity Organization Societies, or COSs, developed in response to these urgent and unmet needs. The COSs provided "friendly visitors," who were usually members of the well-off classes of society, to visit and comfort those in need (Bisman, 1994).

During this period in U.S. history, poverty was seen as a personal failure of the poor. More than that, it was seen as a personal *moral* failure. This moral failure required change on the part of the poor, and it became the task of the volunteer members of the Charity Organization Societies to "guide" the poor and needy out of poverty by education and example. Because the "friendly visitors" did not themselves share any of the problems of these early clients, they assumed that theirs was the "right" morality, the "right" way to be. Thus, they attempted to help the poor to become more like themselves.

No matter how hard the "friendly visitors" taught and supported the poor, no matter how hard the poor tried to change, serious problems persisted. With the passage of time, the "friendly visitors" began to realize that it was the social and economic upheavals of the society, rather than the individual moral failures of the person in need, that caused the problems experienced by their clients (Bisman, 1994).

societal not individual

This was an essential shift in the profession's view of the population it served. No longer was the goal to "save" the poor by "making them more like us." Rather, it became a commitment to work with, and possibly to change, the circumstances in which the poor and vulnerable found themselves. This refocused the mission of the profession to reflect a broader and more comprehensive view of the problems it was committed to address.

During this period, the growth and expansion of the profession, and the shift in its perception of its function, was recognized by the society as a whole, as well as by professionals in other fields. Recognition was gained for the unique body of knowledge, skills, and interventions social workers could provide in addressing an ever-expanding variety of problems in social functioning.

Perhaps the first to recognize the unique expertise of social workers were physicians, who found that social workers could be helpful in assisting patients to plan for community care after an illness and/or hospitalization (Lubove, 1965). Social workers were accustomed to going into communities and were knowledgeable about the resources that existed. They were also skilled in working with families and were able to help physicians to ensure proper family support for patients. Social workers could also provide services within the hospital setting itself, assisting physicians in assessing the social and psychological problems associated with the illness of their patients; thus, medical social work was born.

physician assistants

Teachers also appreciated the expertise of social workers and welcomed them into the school setting, where they could work with students and their families, making home visits to assess the impact of the home on school performance and behavior (Hodge, 1917). Psychiatric settings began to use social workers to gather information about patients, their families, and their preadmission circumstances, as well as to ensure support and supervision for patients after discharge in their communities (Lubove, 1965).

Teachers

The work of the Charity Organization Societies laid the groundwork for the formation of family and children's agencies as they exist today. The dual focus that remains was traditionally a part of these early agencies as well: a focus on effecting change in the individual to promote better functioning and a focus on effecting change in the environment to better support the individual. Agency-based, client-centered social work became known as "social casework," which today is referred to as clinical social work or "micro" practice—a process of assessment and change via interventions on various levels, in order to improve the functioning of the individual.

The Settlement House Movement

Successive waves of European immigrants came to the eastern United States seeking freedom, opportunity, space, and a release from the economic and political woes of their native countries during the nineteenth and early twentieth centuries. In this country, many of these immigrants believed (as did the Hispanics, Asians, and other immigrant groups that continued to follow) the streets were paved with gold and anything was possible.

Some of these immigrants landed and kept on going, eventually settling the vast open spaces of the midwest and western states. Most, however, congregated in the large urban centers of the East Coast, often not far from the very spot where they first set foot in the "New World." There, the majority found that the streets were not paved with gold but with poverty, hard work, disease, and want of every kind.

Conditions were often as crowded, if not more so, as they had been in the lands that they had left. Immigrants did not speak the new language, did not have the skills needed and desired in this country, and had customs and habits alien to the resident population. They came from different cultures, religions, and ethnicities: they *looked* different, they *acted* differently, and they *believed* differently.

These differences, as well as the economic conditions in the United States, increased the hardships new immigrants faced. Prejudice and discrimination forced them into menial jobs at low pay and provided poor housing, medical care, and educational systems. As each of the successive waves worked to improve their condition, new waves arrived to take their places at the bottom of the social and economic ladder. *[handwritten margin note: cyclical]*

A few longtime residents whose eyes were open to the poverty and distress of immigrant populations set up organizations to help them and to attempt to bring about change in the social conditions they encountered. They bought houses in the poorer areas of cities where immigrants lived, which became known as "settlement houses."

Many concerned volunteers themselves came to live in these houses, among the population they wished to serve. There, they attempted to provide whatever services they found to be needed in the community: English lessons, social opportunities, counseling and advising to youth and families, cooking and marketing classes, exploration of job opportunities, and assistance in preparation for interviews are only a few examples of the services provided by settlement house workers.

The Neighborhood Guild of New York was the first of such settlement houses, and many, many others followed (Davis, 1967). Hull House, in Chicago, where Jane Addams lived and worked, is a famous example, and her book *Twenty Years at Hull House* is a classic (Addams, 1910). In addition to providing direct services, settlement houses also advocated for social reforms on behalf of the residents of the communities they were serving.

Grounded in the settlement house tradition, such fields of practice as group work, social advocacy, social reform, and community organization developed. Today, we find that the need for these kinds of services has become even more urgent, as ever-larger portions of the general population remain vulnerable and oppressed. Along with these, the new immigrants, refugees, and undocumented aliens of the 1990s continue to need the very services that the settlement house workers provided. This macro level of practice encompasses social legislation, advocacy, policy and planning, and administration, as well as social action and change.

Macro

Social Work Today

The richness and variation found in our profession today are derived from the concern and commitment of early social workers to the populations for whom they felt a very special care and obligation: the poor, the vulnerable, and the oppressed—those without a voice, without opportunities, without the living conditions our society believes are a necessary component of a dignified and meaningful human life.

As a profession, we argue whether private practice is a mark of "professionalization" or personal selfishness, whether "micro" or "macro" practice should be the primary focus in professional education, whether managed care could, or should, affect the way we practice, whether the homeless wandering our streets are really "clients," whether our "primary" obligation is to the client in our office or the society as a whole, and many other important issues. We struggle with advocacy and with whether the profession can, or should, speak with one voice on difficult issues, such as abortion, gay rights, euthanasia, or the rights of noncitizens.

Within these discussions and debates there is strength: They are signs that the profession is continuing its work of defining itself within an ever-changing societal framework. Far from viewing such work on self-definition as a weakness, one can view it instead as a sign that the social work profession, along with society in general and the world of nature all around us, is still evolving. Evolution is a natural condition, a process that emerges from the condition of living. Thus, as a profession, we are "alive" and "well."

One feature that seems to remain constant within all of the discussions and debates is the profession's original, special commitment: its responsibility toward oppressed and vulnerable populations. As a profession we each, singly and together, make the commitment to this segment of our society a central concern.

Ethical Perspective

Professional codes of ethics assist professions to develop and define standards of practice for members. They are also a means through which the society within which the profession is practiced may assess and understand both the profession as a whole and individual practitioners within it. Codes set standards that reflect the mission and purpose of the profession as a whole.

The need for a professional code of ethics for social workers was first noted by the American Association of Social Workers, the major professional social work organization of its day, in 1924, but a code was not written and adopted by the organization until 1951. When, in the mid-1950s, all professional organizations for social workers joined together under the name of National Association of Social Workers, work was immediately begun on a code of ethics. A code of ethics for social workers was formally adopted in 1960 and has been revised and updated periodically since that time (Loewenberg & Dolgoff, 1992).

The most recent revision of the code was accepted in 1996 by the Delegate Assembly of the National Association of Social Workers. Its provisions became binding upon professional social workers at all levels as of January 1997.

In accordance with the historical mission of the profession as developed in the preceding section of this chapter, the code of ethics reflects a special mission of the profession to action on behalf of oppressed and vulnerable populations. It is useful to review those sections of the code that specifically address these issues in order to understand each worker's personal professional obligations in this regard.

This obligation is addressed immediately in the code's mission statement, the first sentence of which is included here:

> The primary mission of the social work profession is to enhance human well-being, and help meet the basic human needs of all people, with particular attention to the needs and empowerment of people who are vulnerable, oppressed, and living in poverty. (Preamble, NASW Code of Ethics, p. 1)

In the second paragraph, this concept is expanded to include a personal commitment:

> Social workers are sensitive to cultural and ethnic diversity and strive to end discrimination, oppression, poverty, and other forms of social injustice. (Preamble, NASW Code of Ethics, p. 1)

Social justice itself is defined as one of the six core values of the profession and leads to the formulation of the Ethical Principle, which states that "Social workers challenge social injustice." This obligation is described as the following:

> Social workers pursue social change, particularly with and on behalf of vulnerable and oppressed individuals and groups of people. Social workers' change efforts are focused primarily on issues of poverty, unemployment, discrimination and other forms of social injustice. These activities seek to promote sensitivity to and knowledge about oppression and cultural and ethnic diversity. (Ethical Principles, NASW Code of Ethics, p. 5)

There are several sections of the Ethical Standards of the code that refer to this obligation more specifically. These are presented to assist you in clarifying the profession's commitment and in considering your own responsibility within that commitment.

1.05 (b)   Social workers should have a knowledge base of their clients' cultures and be able to demonstrate competence in the provision of services that are sensitive to clients' cultures and to differences among people and cultural groups.

(c)   Social workers should obtain education about and seek to understand the nature of social diversity and oppression with respect to race, ethnicity, national origin, color, sex, sexual orientation, age, marital status, political belief, religion, and mental or physical disability. (p. 9).

4.02   Social workers should not practice, condone, facilitate, or collaborate with any form of discrimination on the basis of race, ethnicity, national origin, color, sex, sexual orientation, age, marital status, political belief, religion, or mental or physical disability. (p. 22)

6.04 (a)   Social workers should engage in social and political action that seeks to ensure that all people have equal access to the resources, employment, services and opportunities they require to meet their basic human needs and to develop fully . . .

(b)   Social workers should act to expand choice and opportunity for all people with special regard for vulnerable, disadvantaged, oppressed, and exploited people and groups.

(c)   Social workers should promote conditions that encourage respect for cultural and social diversity within the United States and globally. Social workers should promote policies and practices that demonstrate respect for difference, support the expansion of cultural knowledge and resources, advocate for programs and institutions that demonstrate cultural competence, and promote policies that safeguard the rights of and conform equity and social justice for all people.

(d)   Social workers should act to prevent and eliminate domination of, exploitation of, and discrimination against any person, group, or class on the basis of race, ethnicity, national origin, color, sex, sexual orientation, age, marital status, political belief, religion, or mental and physical disability.

In its Statement of Purpose, the code includes the following:

Social workers should also be aware of the impact on ethical decision-making of their clients' and *their own personal values and cultural and religious beliefs and practices.* [author's emphasis] (Purpose, NASW Code of Ethics, p. 3)

Understanding one's own "personal values and cultural and religious beliefs" is a complex and difficult task, which involves a willingness to inquire deeply into personal beliefs and life experiences. However, commitment to the profession demands that this process be undertaken by each social worker on an individual basis. Gaining insight and self-awareness in the area of one's own values and biases in regard to the at-risk, vulnerable, disempowered, and oppressed populations that form the central focus of the professional endeavor is a lifelong task. This workbook is meant to assist you to begin this difficult but ultimately rewarding process of self-discovery.

Chapter Exercise

With an understanding of the history of the profession, and its special commitment to at-risk and disempowered populations expressed in the NASW Code of Ethics, describe the qualities that would enable a social worker to provide skilled, empathic, and appropriate service to these populations?

Chapter TWO

Merging Personal and Professional Goals

Chapter 1 has explored the mission and goals of the profession from both a historical and an ethical perspective. The special commitment of the profession to work with poor, vulnerable, and oppressed populations has been clarified, and the responsibility that this commitment places upon each social work professional defined. In this chapter, we will consider the manner in which these professional commitments and our own personal motivation toward the social work profession come together.

Professional Goals

As professionals, we have an ethical responsibility to approach the profession's overall commitment to oppressed and vulnerable populations with sensitivity, concern, and care. This sensitivity must be drawn from knowledge and understanding of the history of these populations prior to immigration, and of their experiences in the United States. History and experience shapes each group's understanding of themselves and the wider society. In addition, we must be knowledgeable about the culture and belief system that exists within each group. We must also be sensitive to differences in attitudes and beliefs about asking for help and about the helping process.

Interested professionals may broaden their knowledge by reading material by, for, and about the particular population they wish to understand. They may attend community, cultural, or religious events and learn about group members' experiences. They may learn about oppression theories and integrate this learning with their general knowledge of vulnerable and oppressed populations. They may learn about a population's worldview, the window through which it regards self and others. This knowledge, as well as skills in culturally competent planning, interviewing, assessment, and evaluation are necessary for competent professional practice.

A good knowledge and skill base is a necessary precondition to ethical and responsible practice with oppressed populations. However, this base is necessary but not sufficient in rendering competent professional service.

Knowledge of a population, as well as the identification and use of appropriate techniques, is generally an *intellectual* enterprise. The professional may maintain a distance from the population during this process. The population is still a "they"—something other, different, unusual. The values, beliefs, and experiences of the population are not necessarily related to the values and experiences of each social worker.

"They" are understood in a manner that the worker believes to be "objective"—separate from the person of the worker. However, we must recognize that such "objectivity" cannot and does not, in fact, exist. Rather, each worker receives and processes information about other populations through the lens of her own life experiences, goals, and worldview.

Thus, the obligation set forth in the NASW Code of Ethics to an understanding of "personal values and cultural and religious beliefs" takes on a new meaning and asks for another level of commitment to knowledge and understanding from social workers. This knowledge and understanding is no longer only about "other." It is about self, and it is, at least in part, an *affective* enterprise.

Personal Goals

Knowledge of self is a vast and complex enterprise, one that involves a lifetime of commitment. Self-knowledge is an important dimension of education for the social work profession, and an ongoing obligation for professionals in the field. Just as the profession recognizes the important impact of each client's worldview; life experience; cultural, ethnic, and religious beliefs; and personal value system on his or her perception of his or her life situation and problems, so it also recognizes that these same dimensions in the social worker will affect his or her views of the client's problems and possible resolutions to those problems.

Self-awareness in all dimensions is beyond the scope of the present enterprise. It is recognized that a seemingly limitless number of life experiences and beliefs may affect professional work. This workbook shall assist the reader to consider a part of these experiences and beliefs only—those that most strongly affect work with populations toward whom the profession has a special commitment.

Exploring Your Motivation for the Profession

We may begin this task by exploring our reasons for entering the profession. These are generally drawn from our own philosophical and ethical perspective. This exploration will help to define the unique worldview we each bring into the social work profession.

It is generally understood that people entering professions, particularly the service professions, have a commitment to something broader than the provision of a reasonable source of income, although the importance of this cannot be disclaimed. Professional education is often rigorous, and membership in a profession affects the whole person at all times.

There is a sense in which a chosen profession "defines" the individual who "professes" it. Ethical codes and professional standards affect professionals not only in the course of their work, but in all aspects of their lives. A commitment to a profession entails a lifetime and is generally undertaken with care and reflection.

Because commitment to professional practice has such a pervasive effect on the life of each professional, it is important that such a commitment be made with full awareness of one's personal goals, values, and beliefs. If the values and goals of the profession one is considering are similar to the person's personal value and belief system, if they support and enhance each other, this consonance will be extremely helpful to the person throughout the course of her career and will decrease the possibility of conflict between personal goals and professional obligations.

It is recognized that each social worker's reasons for entering the profession are complex and multilayered and that the particular constellation of reasons and motivations is unique to each worker. However, a beginning awareness will be helpful in considering how you view others and yourself in relation to your career choice. You may find that there are several, possibly overlapping, reasons you have chosen social work as your profession.

Some Possible Answers

In the course of years of teaching, many students have been asked, both individually and in the classroom, to consider why they have chosen the social work profession as their career goal. Some of their answers are presented here to assist you in thinking through your own reasons for choosing social work.

"To help others"

The most common answer to this question, by far, is that people choose to enter social work out of a strong desire to help others. This response, though almost universal, is so broad that it may not be helpful to the worker seeking true self-knowledge and self-awareness. To help others, yes, but *why?* Why do *you* want to help others?

Although this question may be answered in various ways, there is another piece hidden within it that may help you to understand professional motivation. Entering a profession "to help others" carries with it the implicit belief that

a. help is possible
b. I can provide the help
c. It is good to help others

Thus, it is an affirmation that growth and change, healing and progress are possible for people in general and, specifically, for people with problems. It is also an affirmation of the individual—I, who am making this choice to become a social worker, believe that I am/will be able to provide this help.

"To save people" (from harm of some sort)

Most of us, we must admit, have at least a touch of the savior instinct. When we look about us, we see people with problems, people in various kinds of danger, and in various kinds of pain, both physical and emotional. Seeing people in danger and pain causes us to feel empathy, sympathy, and a kind of pain of our own. We want to relieve them of their pain and believe that social work interventions will be able to accomplish this.

Implicit in this response is the idea that:

  a. it is possible to relieve pain and suffering

  b. the knowledge base of social work will enable this relief

  c. people who are suffering want help

"To fully live religious obligations"

The Bible is full of injunctions to help others. Being our brother's (or sister's) keeper, loving all people as God loves us, doing God's work, being kind to our neighbors and other clear religious directions help people focus outward from self with understanding and work to help others. There is often a feeling of oneness with the deity that accompanies "doing good works," which unites both the giver and the receiver in a transcendent relationship with the Supreme Being.

It is not necessary to pursue a career in social work to achieve this objective. Involvement in charitable organizations and work may provide a meaningful expression for this desire without the rigors of professional obligation. However, many social workers feel that it is through the skill and knowledge base of the profession that they can be most effective in this work.

Generally, workers who choose this response also accept that

  a. there is a transcendent being

  b. this transcendent being cares about people

  c. caring about people brings me, and those I help, closer to the transcendent

"To heal the world"

Some people look around the world as they know it and see pain and suffering. This pain and suffering is not just at the level of the individual. There is a sense, they feel, in which every person on earth suffers if one person suffers. Thus, alleviating the pain of others helps not only those who may benefit directly, but indirectly helps the whole of humanity.

Some assumptions inherent in this kind of response are

  a. all of humanity is interdependent

  b. helping an individual helps everyone

"Because I can't stand to see other people suffering"

It is difficult to know other people are suffering due to personal or institutional problems that affect their ability to find happiness and fulfillment. More personal than the "to heal the world" response, some people feel that they individually don't have the right to be happy while others are suffering, in need, or in pain. The care of others is necessary before one can allow oneself personal fulfillment and happiness.

This view often includes a commitment to a certain level of need fulfillment for everyone, before anyone has a "right" to a higher level.

Assumptions of this view might include

a. there should be justice and fairness in the world

b. human beings' needs are capable of being met

c. human beings want to find happiness and fulfillment

"Because people always turn to me for help"

Often, people become aware that others seem to "naturally" turn to them for help and advice. They are always willing to listen and to "be there" for people, and they derive satisfaction from knowing that they are able to do this.

Many people recognize this "natural" tendency when friends, acquaintances, and co-workers express their appreciation for the care, concern, and sound advice that they have received. They may feel that they have been given this natural ability as a gift, and therefore, it is their personal obligation to use it to help others. Acquiring the skills and competence of a social work professional enables them to accomplish this task by relying upon a recognized knowledge base rather than "instinct."

Inherent in this kind of response is the feeling that

a. I have a special ability that was given to me

b. I must use this ability to help others

c. Becoming a social worker will enable me to do this.

"Because I love to talk"

As a profession, we are a verbal and often very talkative group. We enjoy conversation and verbal expression. Some people believe that they can put this love of talking and communication to work to help others. It is a skill that they enjoy using and think that it would be wonderful to be able to spend the day talking to people and doing good for others besides!

This kind of response may also be saying that

a. it is possible to help others through verbal communication

b. I enjoy communicating, and want to use it for helping others

c. The knowledge base of social work will help me achieve helpful communication with those in need.

"Because I'm curious"

I have spoken to many professionals who say that they especially enjoy learning "what makes people tick." They enjoy exploring the infinite variations of human nature and helping others toward their own unique fulfillment.

Some people describe others as "a beautiful package, that I slowly unwrap," (taking care, of course, to be very careful and respectful in the unwrapping). All people are beautiful packages—we find the beauty and strength in each.

Implicit in this kind of response might be that

a. each individual is unique, special, and valuable

b. I can find enjoyment in discovery of this uniqueness

c. I can help others by doing something I enjoy

"Because I have so much myself"

It is a form of gratefulness, to God or to humanity or to luck or to whatever one believes, to offer help to others. If you believe that you have been fortunate to have been born with, or been able to achieve, the opportunities and gifts that have been given to you, you may feel, out of love and sincere appreciation, the desire to help those less fortunate than yourself.

If you believe that this may be part of your reason for entering the profession, it is very important for you to explore *why* you believe you were blessed in these ways, while others were not. Is it the "luck of the draw"? Is it deserved in some way because of your own or your ancestor's virtues? Is it because of your own acts? The way you answer this question provides insight into your feelings about oppressed and vulnerable populations.

Underlying this response might be ideas that

- **a.** having or not having is (always)(sometimes)(never) deserved or undeserved

- **b.** it is an expression of gratefulness to assist those less fortunate

- **c.** I'm willing to share my resources with others

"Because I had such a hard time myself, and no one was there for me"

Some of us have had painful and difficult life experiences. Added to that pain was loneliness and a sense of abandonment—a feeling that no one was there and no one cared. Aware of how this felt, we want to help others to have a different experience, to "be there" for them as no one was for us.

Severe traumas like these may leave scars buried deeply within, scars that we still carry today. They may make us especially kind, empathetic, and thoughtful social workers, but they may also impede our understanding of the unique and different situations our clients bring to us.

Some possible assumptions here are

- **a.** someone should "be there" for people when they need help

- **b.** someone who "is there" for someone else will be able to help

- **c.** my own experiences will help me to help others

"Because I had such a hard time myself, and someone was there for me"

I want to return the favor and be there for someone else. Many people today have, at some point in their lives, received help of some kind. When we have received help, we often can recognize the value of someone being there to help in times of distress.

Perhaps we admired this person and seek to emulate her or him. Perhaps we just want to give back to others what we have received, out of gratefulness. We might have recognized the special skills that enabled someone to help us and valued those skills. Becoming a professional means, in part, acquiring these same skills.

Some possible underlying ideas here might include

- **a.** I have received: therefore, I should give

- **b.** the help that worked for me can help others

"Because I just like people"

It is probable that everyone in social work would choose this answer. It is a given of the profession: liking people in general is a reasonable prerequisite for working with them meaningfully and well.

Many assumptions can underlie this kind of statement. A few possibilities follow:

    a. All people are/can be likeable to me.

    b. All people are worthy of care, dignity, respect, concern, etc.

    c. I will find meaning in relating to any person.

    d. I prefer working with people to working with things or working alone.

"Because I think relationships with coworkers are important, and I enjoy relating to social workers."

We've all known people who are unhappy at work because of poor relationships with colleagues, or because of the general atmosphere of competition, antagonism, harassment, or distance that pervades their workplace. Indeed, we may even have *been* one of those unhappy people! We believe that social work is different in this regard.

Assumptions here include the following:

    a. All, or most, social workers are nice people who are easy to get along with.

    b. Good relationships with coworkers are important to all, or most, social workers.

    c. As a social worker, I will have good relationships with co-workers.

Assessing Your Personal Answer

This brief and *very* unempirical look at some of the reasons given for entering the profession will help readers explore their own reasons fully, to look behind the sometimes trite and conventional answers to reveal the truth.

We all choose to become social work professionals for altruistic reasons. People entering the helping professions generally state altruistic reasons for so doing. However, we must look further for true self-awareness and understanding.

Looking beneath the conventional answers may be a painful process. It's easier to just stay with the generic "I like to help others." However, a deeper and clearer assessment of our own motivation can be very helpful in beginning the task of achieving self-awareness in relation to vulnerable and oppressed populations.

It is certain that, as you identify your goals and motivations, you will see the commonality between your reasons for wanting to be a social worker and the profession's goals, values, and mission. This commonality is a source of strength that will help to support you through the difficult task that lies before us.

Chapter Exercise

Review your answers to the Chapter 1 exercise. Using these answers as a framework, place your personal goals in entering the social work profession within the context of the profession's mission. What are the differences? The similarities? How can you use your personal goals to strengthen the mission of the profession?

Chapter THREE

Disempowerment and the Professional Encounter

All societal groups function within a culture: a set of beliefs and attitudes, norms and values, traditions and behavior styles. Cultures enable members to meet their biological and psychological needs (Pinderhughes, 1989, p. 6).

Minority groups, oppressed groups, at-risk groups, vulnerable groups, and others have developed cultures that support their efforts to meet their needs within society. Each population's culture is unique in certain ways, as the qualities of that population are unique. However, oppressed populations' cultures often share common elements as well, for they share a common need: they must interact with the dominant society in which they exist.

Learning One's "Place" in the World

We all are shaped by the particular circumstances in which we find ourselves. Family and community, school, church, and peer group all have an enormous impact on the development of people in terms of their understanding of the world and their place in it.

As we grow, we experience joy and happiness, creativity and achievement, relationship and aloneness, sorrow and grief, anger, suffering, pain, love, and hate. We find that some experiences reinforce older ones and seem to occur with some regularity, while others stand alone, seemingly unique and different. Some of us learn to avoid or deflect experiences that are painful and unpleasant, or to minimize them. Others of us may find these experiences so overwhelming that they leave us helpless and unable to act.

We are each a part of society and are affected strongly and intimately by the social institutions that surround us. Each of us interacts with them in some way on a daily basis. Some of us find these institutions supportive of our life experiences and the things we have learned from them. Others find that negative and unpleasant experiences occur in interactions with certain kinds of societal institutions, such as schools, the justice system, and social services. The negative experiences associated with societal institutions occur over and over again, creating a kind of a "fight or flight" reaction in us. In response, we learn to be on guard and defensive.

We are also affected by our individual interactions with others. We enjoy experiences with others who treat us positively and with respect. We do not enjoy, and learn to avoid, experiences with people whose interaction with us reveals negative feelings, power and dominance, lack of respect, fear, and hatred. Sometimes we may notice similarities in treatment and become aware that positive experiences seem to develop from interactions with particular *kinds* of people: children, African Americans, Moslems, rural families, Christians, Japanese, Irish, males, college-educated people, working class people, etc. In the same way, we learn to associate negative experiences with other *kinds* of people.

Thus, we learn to categorize: some people like us and make us feel positive when we are with them, and some people do not and arouse negative feelings. We do the same with institutions: we feel positive when we interact with the grocery store on the corner, and negative in the impersonal supermarket, no matter how much wider the offerings. We learn to meet our shopping needs at the corner store. We feel positive when we are in math class and negative in English class. We learn to love math and to avoid English.

These are natural processes, a part of normal socialization. They continue throughout our lives except that, as we avoid and separate ourselves from the circumstances where our experiences have been negative, we close off entire areas of potential experiences. As we get older, some of us protect ourselves as best we can and live within our circumscribed circle of "good" potential experiences, rarely taking risks with the unknown and possible negative experiences.

The amount, or degree, of risk we are willing to take in encountering new experiences may be related to countless variables: often, there is a component of personal assessment of "the odds," based on associated previous experiences.

Humankind is social: we live with and around others. We learn to see ourselves as members of a certain "group," based on similarities and differences we define as important. Our life experiences and our need to categorize lead us to group ourselves by age, race, class, religion, ethnic origin, region, interests, occupations, and other dimensions. We may perceive ourselves as belonging to many different, overlapping groups or predominately to one group. The way we see ourselves in terms of personal and group affiliations helps us to form that part of our character that we call our identity. Theories of identity development will be presented in Chapter 5.

The Professional Encounter

As Reamer states:

> The conditions that cause people to seek help from social workers and social services are invariably consequences of oppression and injustice. . . . While not all social and emotional difficulties that bring people to social services would

immediately vanish were oppression and injustice eliminated, many certainly would. (Reamer, 1994, p. 257)*

Human service delivery systems are never culture-free: the programs and institutions are reflective of the culture in which they are embedded; and providers of services, such as social workers, are similarly embedded in their own culture. Pinderhughes views the effects of cultural difference as having an enormous impact on service delivery:

> The differences between client and practitioner in values, norms, beliefs, lifestyles, and life opportunities extend to every aspect of the health, mental health, and social services delivery system, which itself is a cultural phenomenon. The programming of service delivery, the structuring of services for people, the engagement of patients and clients in the help-giving process, the degree to which people use services, the assessment and treatment of problems, and the evaluation of outcomes are all in some way influenced by cultural values and traditions. For clients and patients, culture determines what they see as a problem, how they express it, whom they seek out for help, what they regard as helpful, and the treatment strategies they prefer. For practitioners, culture also defines what is seen as a problem, how this is expressed, who can provide help, and what treatment options may be considered. (Pinderhughes, 1989, p. 13)**

Chapters 1 and 2 of this workbook have addressed the commitment of the profession to oppressed and disempowered populations and your own commitment in terms of why you selected social work as a profession. The importance of self-awareness in terms of this work has been an underlying theme.

Differences between the worker and the client in culture and worldview have a strong impact on the client–worker relationship. These differences are particularly important because of the imbalances inherent in the relationship: of "giving" and of "taking" help, of power and authority, and of knowledge. Thus, your awareness of your own culture, and of its particular set of values and beliefs, biases and prejudices becomes more urgent. In this chapter, we will explore some of these elements in the context of the client–worker relationship.

The client–worker relationship develops and is sustained through a process of mutual communication, both verbal and non-verbal. Communication between people is complex. We begin with a sender, who has something to transmit. That "something" must be encoded (through word, touch, expression, etc.), then transmitted to the receiver. The transmission must be received (heard, read, seen, felt), then decoded and acknowledged (Shulman, 1992, p. 53).

It is easy to see how errors, miscommunications, and failed communications can occur with such a process. When the communication is about difficult or sensitive matters; is between individuals who do not necessarily share a common history, culture, language, experience, or knowledge base;

*From *Foundations of Social Work Knowledge* by Fred Reamer. Copyright © 1994 by Columbia University Press. Reprinted with permission of the publisher.

**From *Understanding Race, Ethnicity, and Power: The Key to Efficacy in Clinical Practice* by Elaine Pinderhughes. Copyright © 1989 by The Free Press, a Division of Simon & Schuster. Reprinted with permission of the publisher.

is contained within a relationship that is not inherently equal; and contains a strong affective component; the potential for problems increases.

No relationship between two human beings can be fully equal in all respects. Differences may be as diverse as physical strength, education, intelligence, breadth of experience, perceptiveness, position in society, financial status, access to resources, specific skills or talent, and an infinity of others. Thus, every relationship with another person contains some imbalances and adjusts itself to them or compensates for them in some manner. The relationship between client and worker contains, in addition, some specific imbalances drawn from the difference between asking and giving help, and from knowledge, authority, and power differences.

"Power," Pinderhughes states, "is critical to one's mental health. *Everyone* needs it" (Pinderhughes, 1989, p. 110).

Our Clients' Experiences

Clients bring their whole selves with them to the helping process: they bring all of their group affiliations, biopsychosocial histories, and current functioning. Each aspect, and each affiliation, affects the client in some way. Particularly, the client's primary group affiliations—family, peers, friends, and coworkers—affect and modify her or his perceptions of her- or himself and the helping process that is about to occur (Kadushin, 1990, p. 67–68).

Thus, it is important for the worker to understand and acknowledge the influence of the client's identity, worldview and culture, the context in which the client's problem is embedded, and the potential suspicion and lack of trust that the client may bring to the helping process. These factors are greatly enhanced by minority group or at-risk status (Meyer & Mattaini, 1995, p. 44).

Clients come for help at a particular time, to a particular agency or resource, and become "our" clients when assigned to work with us. Depending on our agency's mission and purpose, we may know already that our client has a particular kind of problem or belongs to a particular group of people. Even when this is so, we know that it is best to approach our client with an open mind and a minimum of presuppositions. This is a part of our professional value base, and guides our practice.

In the process of professional education, social workers learn about establishing relationships, maintaining trust and confidentiality, and specific interviewing and assessment techniques. We approach clients with all of our knowledge and skill. We recognize that our clients are strongly affected by their life experiences and their group and individual identities. We also recognize that clients are affected by their perception of our own individual and group identities.

Imbalances Inherent in "Asking" for Help

There are several kinds of imbalances inherent in the relationship between client and social worker. A primary one is drawn from the reason the worker and client are together: the client has a problem and is asking the worker for help. The client is the *subject* of the work that is to be done. The worker enables, suggests, assists, and mandates change in the client.

The client erroneously assumes that the worker remains unchanged by the client–worker relationship. The change that is to occur, the client believes, is in the client only. Asking for help in itself creates a condition of vulnerability which is exacerbated by the client's belief that the worker does not need help. Further, the worker may give or deny help and may place conditions on it that the client may be forced to accept.

Circumstances may have placed the client in the position of asking for help many times. The client may feel dependent and helpless, unable to act on her own behalf. Experience with oppression and disempowerment may have made the client feel hopeless about acting for herself, unsure of her own opinions, and lacking in confidence in her own ability to address her problems. It is important for the worker to be aware of the potential for such feelings and their effects on the developing client–worker relationship.

Power, Authority, and Knowledge Imbalances

Power and authority issues are always present in the helping relationships. The worker carries power and authority from two sources: (1) power and authority is drawn from the institutional aspect—the agency's purpose and program and the worker's function within that; (2) power and authority is drawn from psychological considerations—clients give these to workers based on the worker's presumed knowledge, expertise, and ability to help the client with problems. Thus, many clients are willing to accept the power imbalances. Workers who recognize this are able to provide a relationship that enables change in a safe and secure environment. However, in some circumstances, clients may be adversely affected by their own feelings about power, authority, and knowledge imbalances (Compton & Galway, 1989, p. 295–96).

Although in many circumstances workers try to minimize the disequilibrium in knowledge, authority, and power between themselves and clients through the use of specific skills and techniques such as empathy, positive regard, and warmth and genuineness, clients are very much aware of this imbalance. While it is perhaps most obvious in work with mandated clients, even relationships characterized by informality, such as the use of first names, informal dress, and casual meeting places, contain imbalances of which clients are aware.

The social worker must understand that the client's response to this disequilibrium will be affected by her previous experiences with similar circumstances, perhaps with teachers, police, other social workers, or parents. An exploration of these issues and experiences may be helpful in engaging the client fully in the process of change and growth. This task is most difficult, of course, with nonvoluntary clients, where power and authority may need to become a part of the tools used by the worker on the client's behalf.

The client comes to the worker for help because the worker is assumed to have the knowledge necessary to provide the help. There are often differences in levels of formal education between client and worker of which both are aware. These may be manifested in manner of speech, behavior, and knowledge base. The worker has a level of expertise she will use to assist the client, and the client assumes he or she does not to have this kind of expertise.

In certain settings, the social worker also has authority over some aspects of the client's life. The worker may control, for example, access to children placed in foster care, or to a spouse, funds for a job skills program, social welfare funding, access to specialized housing, whether probation or parole is recommended, whether a student is removed from a certain school setting, and various other life choices. The authority granted to the social worker limits the freedom of the client. If the client does not comply with the social worker's plan, there will be consequences in the client's life.

The social worker functions within a social contract: society and societal institutions have given the worker this kind of power. Because of this, the client identifies the social worker with the dominant members of society. This identification tends to occur even if the worker is a member of a disempowered and/or oppressed group. In the professional role, the worker represents the power of society over the client. Power, Pinderhughes says, carries with it

> associations of dominance, superiority, and denigration. . . . is embodied in both cultural dynamics and the clinical role. (Pinderhughes, 1990, p. 109)

Where the worker clearly belongs to a dominant cultural, ethnic, racial, religious, or other group, these differences are powerful considerations for the client. Thus, they become vital elements to consider in the development of the client–worker relationship.

Despite all of the previously mentioned elements, there is a level at which the client maintains control. The client can, after all, accept or reject help, participate in the process or remain silent, share information or refuse to share, and follow an intervention or treatment plan or ignore, subvert, or reject it. The price of such ultimate control may be high—in certain circumstances, this may involve separation from partner, loss of contact with children, or incarceration—but the potential for power on the part of the client remains.

Our Own Experiences

Social workers, like clients, bring their whole selves to the encounter as well: reference groups, primary group affiliations, history and current functioning. However, as trained professionals, workers attempt to minimize the effect of affiliations and history on the professional encounter (Kadushin, 1990, p. 68–69).

It is impossible to completely eliminate all effects of one's life experiences, culture, affiliations, and history on the social work encounter. However, self-awareness will assist workers in this endeavor, helping them to recognize when their beliefs and attitudes are affecting the helping process in a negative manner. Identification with professional goals and values, and a thorough grounding in theoretical frameworks will assist the worker as well.

Worker and client approach the relationship with differing expectations, motivations, and goals. Workers have *chosen* to be social work professionals, perhaps for some of the reasons discussed in Chapter 2. Their expectation is that the client–worker contact not only will be helpful to the client but will be a positive experience for themselves. In most cases, the decision to become a social worker was made without coercion of any kind.

The worker is aware that there are imbalances in the client–worker relationship, and knows that these imbalances need to be acknowledged and addressed to promote a sustained positive working relationship with a client. The worker is also aware that the client entering such a relationship may be strongly affected by previous experiences with "the system" of societal institutions. The client initially views the worker through the lens of these experiences. Their effect on the current relationship must be understood. If negative, they must be addressed in order to create the potential for a positive experience, if positive, they must be addressed so that realistic expectations for the current relationship can be established.

Imbalances Inherent in "Giving" Help

There is a gift that comes with receiving help. There is a gift that comes with giving help as well: the gift of feeling good about being helpful, competent, knowledgeable, and skillful, and able to make a difference in someone's life. These positive feelings and experiences affect the way we work with clients.

Studies have shown that in settings where workers do not receive much positive feedback from clients, and/or where work is filled with stress, potential danger, anxiety, and tension, workers tend to suffer from burnout. We need the satisfaction of accomplishing something, of a job well done. Often, we rely on our client's words and actions to give us this feedback.

Thus, social workers have strong investments in the "success" of their work. We *want* our client's problems to resolve or improve, so we can feel that we have accomplished something of value. However, many social workers also find that there is another, more painful and negative, side to the imbalance that occurs with giving help to others.

It is not uncommon for our clients to become dependent on us for intervention, advice, support, and resources. There is a part of us that values the feelings that come with the client's dependence. This is where our "savior" image flourishes. We may feel that our clients need us and can't manage without us. We might feel that it is our work with clients that keeps them functioning.

This overemphasis on the need that our client has for our own personal, individual, and unique help makes it difficult to terminate or to transfer clients, and it can blur a worker's perception of client strengths and abilities. Instead of working from an empowerment model, social workers at times may encourage and foster dependence by the client. Clients often comply, either due to their own personal needs, or to the belief that workers represent society and societal norms.

Fostering this kind of a relationship with a client may be ultimately detrimental to the overall objective of every intervention: to help individuals develop to their highest potential. It may be even more destructive in working with clients who are habitually disempowered and oppressed by societal institutions, because it reinforces the validity of the oppression and causes these clients to feel even greater degrees of powerlessness, vulnerability, and lack of control over the circumstances of their lives.

Power, Authority, and Knowledge Imbalances

Social workers are well aware that they possess a knowledge and skill base capable of assisting clients to address their problems. After all, we all worked hard to achieve this competence! It is, indeed, the principal tool that we use in the helping relationship. However, it is difficult to avoid the awareness of the advantages that this knowledge and skill give us.

Our clients tell us of an experience that troubles them. They are focused on the experience. We keep focused with them, while at the same time, stepping back to examine the broader picture. How does this experience fit in with what we know about this client? About this *type* of experience or problem? About this *kind* of client's coping skills? We are able to generalize from specific to general and back again, bringing to our responses a level of insight that we hope will help the client move forward in understanding, growth, and change. This awareness of our professional knowledge can create a separation and an imbalance between ourselves and our clients.

Often, social workers have authority over certain spheres of clients' lives. This is openly a part of workers' relationships with nonvoluntary clients and must always be addressed with them. Even with voluntary clients, however, there is an imbalance in authority that is one of the dynamics of the relationship. Because the worker has expertise in working with the client's problem, it is assumed by both that the worker's interpretation and recommendations carry the weight of authority. Workers strive to work within the client's perception of the problem definition, goals, and interventions and treatments. However, in cases where there is a difference of opinion between client and worker, it is generally the worker's authority that is accepted by both.

The worker is usually aware of this authority and tries to minimize the effect in many circumstances. However, there are times and circumstances where the worker believes that authority must be used. These generally center around "best interest" judgments where client and worker differ regarding desirable outcomes. Because "best interest" is always a subjective determination, it is not unusual for there to be differences between a client and a worker in determining "best interest." The worker, often unaware of the individual issues, judgments, and worldview that affect her or his own determination of "best interest," ultimately is able to exercise authority to impose this personal perception on the client.

Power imbalances between client and worker are obvious to both. The client operates within the choices and power structure available to her or him. The worker may be able to control some of the client's choices in a variety of ways: by denying access to necessary information and resources, by encouraging dependency, by coercion anywhere along the continuum of weak to strong.

The worker believes that she or he uses power justifiably in the interests of the client. She or he also believes that this power has been given to her or him on the basis of proven competence and knowledge by society. Often, however, the power is often used by the worker to assure the client's compliance with the dominant societal norms.

Social work as a profession has had, and continues to have, a difficult time with power and authority. Some workers try to pretend that the power differential does not exist and that they and their clients are, indeed, equal in power. This can create an atmosphere of mistrust as clients wonder why workers attempt to deny what is so obvious to them (Compton & Galway, 1989). However, workers are often uncomfortable with the juxtaposition of the reality of their power and authority and the value concepts of social justice, respect, dignity, and equality foundational to the profession.

As professional social workers, we need to be very aware of both the client's and our own feelings about the power, authority, and knowledge differential. We need to address it openly with clients so that it may be used as a positive element in the helping process. To do this effectively requires self-awareness: not only understanding and knowledge of the power itself, but of our own feelings about, and experiences with, power.

Chapter Exercise

Think of a situation or circumstance in which you felt a strong power imbalance between yourself and another person. This person may have had authority over some aspect of your life, which gave him or her some control over your happiness and life satisfaction, as well as over the achievement of your personal goals and desires. The person may have used the authority and power to assist you or provide you with something, or they may have used it to prevent you from achieving something you wanted.

Write the experience in as much detail as possible, chronicling the "objective" events.

Reread and reflect on what you have written, and allow yourself to reexperience the feelings that you had at that moment about the other person, the circumstances, and yourself. When you have recalled the moment affectively as well as intellectually, write some of the feelings you experienced.

My Experience

My Reactions

Chapter FOUR

A Brief Look at Client Populations

At first glance, *vulnerable, at-risk, disempowered,* and *oppressed populations* seem to be clear descriptive terms. However, they need to be separated from each other in order to facilitate understanding. This chapter will explore each of these terms used here, and attempt to clarify and distinguish between them.

"Population" Implies a Shift from "Case" to "Class"

Chapter 3 explored the power, authority, and knowledge imbalances between social workers and their clients, as well as the imbalance created by the process of asking and giving help itself. Whether the "client" referred to was an individual, a family, a group of adolescents or elderly, or a particular community, the emphasis was on direct relationships with a specific, identified individual or group. This individualized focus encouraged an examination of the specifics of the client-worker experience.

When we speak about "population," however, we are making a major shift. The emphasis moves from the particular personal qualities, patterns, and problems of the client to the characteristic qualities, patterns, and problems that particular client shares with a large number of people—a "population." We lose some of the individuality in the process of focusing, instead, on the commonalities the client shares with a particular group with which he identifies or is identified. We gain a general understanding of a *group* of people.

Vulnerable and At-Risk Populations

Vulnerable clients, according to Gitterman are overwhelmed by "circumstances and events they are powerless to control."

Vulnerable or at-risk populations may be defined as groups of people whose disabilities or impediments leave them more open to harm than other members of the population. The disabilities or impediments are severe, long term, and not amenable to cure, often lasting a lifetime. Vulnerability may be a result of physical, mental, environmental, or emotional problems; societal biases, stereotypes, and prejudices; or a combination of these, and may be due to causes outside of the individual's control.

Vulnerability alone does not ensure that harm will come: only that an increased risk of harm exists for these populations. Many members of vulnerable populations *are* also harmed: they are both vulnerable *and* oppressed.

In working with these at-risk populations, social workers must help clients minimize the potential for harm by building in numerous safeguards. The locus of the work may be within the individual (through supporting and assisting empowerment, increased assertiveness, strengthened coping skills) and/or within the environment (ensuring safety and protection, using community resources, initiating community action and legislation).

Jack Rothman's (1994) *Practice with Highly Vulnerable Clients* defines four populations as vulnerable—at-risk long term and in need of special services and consideration. Each of these populations are in circumstances of "profound hardship" (Rothman, 1994, p. 5). Their vulnerabilities exist over a long span of time and create broad and diverse needs:

1. *The Elderly.* This population is increasing as a percentage of the general population, creating a need for increased services. Especially vulnerable are the frail elderly; those with chronic illnesses and conditions, both physical and mental; those with limited financial resources; and those who are isolated from their support networks.

2. *Children.* Children as a population are generally dependent and unable to care for themselves and meet their own needs. This creates dependence on adults and institutions. Children become especially vulnerable where there is divorce, addiction, child abuse, and violence in their family lives.

3. *The Chronically Mentally Ill.* Whether homeless on the streets of our urban centers, housed in large public institutions, or in abusive or neglectful living conditions with other individuals, those with chronic mental illness have little ability to control the events that structure their lives and are at risk from their own behavior, as well as that of others.

4. *The Physically Disabled.* Physical disability in and of itself leaves the individual in a vulnerable and defenseless position. Often unable to meet their own needs, those who are physically disabled must often depend on others for optimal functioning.

When combined with other characteristics that increase risk, such as minority status, members of these four populations are likely to be victimized and oppressed by both individuals and institutions.

Disempowered Populations

In Chapter 3, we considered the effects of imbalances of power between the client and the worker. Such imbalances occur outside of the professional encounter as well. Indeed, each person is often aware of differences in power between self and others.

In a broader societal context, we may say that disempowered populations lack the capacity to have mastery over themselves, others, or nature. People who are disempowered are unable to influence the forces that affect their lives for their own benefit (Pinderhughes, 1989, p. 109–10).

Powerlessness is a painful and humiliating feeling. Each of us has experienced powerlessness during childhood. We are well aware of the power that parents, teachers, and even siblings exercised over us, often against our wills. With reflection, we can recall the anger, the hurt and frustration, and the immobilization that disempowerment brings.

People with power can achieve the results they desire for themselves, whatever they may be. In our society, these are often status, wealth and material possessions, and freedom and independence. Those without power are unable to achieve these results through their own efforts. People of color, the poor, women, immigrants, refugees, and the elderly are examples of populations who have traditionally lacked power in our society.

Some people belong to more than one disempowered group. Being both black and female, immigrant and Hispanic, or elderly and poor, leads to a double victimization. Empowerment of those who are doubly victimized is often a long and difficult process (Pinderhughes, 1989, p. 114).

Vulnerable, At-Risk, and Disempowered Populations Are Oppressed Populations

Vulnerability to harm and inability to protect oneself from such harm due to powerlessness creates an oppressive situation for anyone. Individuals may be oppressed and victimized on the basis of individual circumstances. However, groups of people, or populations, may also be oppressed in our society.

> Oppression refers to relations of domination and exploitation—economic, social, psychologic—between individuals; between social groups and classes within and beyond societies; and, globally, between entire societies. . . . Oppression seems motivated by an intent to exploit, and it results typically in disadvantageous, unjust conditions of living for its victims. (Reamer, 1994, p. 233)

Oppressed populations are usually considered minority populations, although in the case of women, minority status implies something other than lesser numbers. Populations may be assigned to majority or minority status by the dominant population, by societal institutions, and/or by themselves.

Oppressed populations have a history of exclusion, discrimination, violence, and denial of rights which is based on a specific identifying characteristic, such as race, ethnicity, or religion. They experience poverty and social injustice much more frequently than other members of society.

Oppressed populations suffer external marginalization, exclusion and discrimination. Members of oppressed populations also internalize the negative image held by society, often becoming self-destructive and violent against other members of their population.

Populations that experience oppression do not experience it only on an individual basis. Oppressive conditions can be built into the norms, traditions, policies, and laws of society and are then reflected in its institutions. These institutions, created and usually administered by the dominant groups, embody dominant societal norms; thus, they create conditions of oppression. School schedules that do not account for non-Christian holidays; classrooms accessible only by climbing stairs; public notices and instructions written in English and posted in ethnic neighborhoods; community music and art programs that reflect only the European tradition; legal definitions of "family" that exclude nontraditional family groups; social agencies and programs located at a distance from the populations they are purportedly serving and that don't provide transportation for clients and consumers; school facilities based on the taxable income of the population served; assumptions of criminal guilt based on racial or ethnic characteristics; airline seats that do not accommodate differences in size and shape; even public toilet facilities that do not account for the special needs of gender are but a few examples of institutionalized oppression. Oppressed populations often suffer from lack of access to the goods and resources of society and lack of knowledge about their rights to these.

Oppressors often say, with great sincerity, that they are unaware of oppressing others. Reamer states:

> To individuals, groups, classes, and societies that oppress and exploit others, and impose upon them unjust conditions of living, their policies and practices tend to make sense. For in the consciousness of perpetrators of oppression, their attitudes and actions seem, by and large, compatible with the pursuit of socially sanctioned, legitimate goals, and with the internal logic of established social, economic, cultural, and political institutions. (Reamer, 1994, p. 233)

Oppressed Populations in the United States Today

The most pervasive determinant of an oppressed population in our society appears to be race. However, populations are also oppressed due to ethnicity, religion, social class, gender, and other characteristics. A partial list of possible populations that suffer oppression in the United States might include the following:

- **A.** *Race.* White is the dominant race in the United States. Membership, or perceived membership, in another racial group creates an oppressive condition.

- **B.** *Ethnic or National Origin.* Northern Europeans are a numerically small group but are dominant in terms of societal institutions, language, and cultural norms. Immigrant groups in the United States each suffered oppression and discrimination upon entry. The longer a national or ethnic group has been in the United States and the more similar in appearance, language, and customs to the dominant group, the more it is accepted into the "mainstream." The exception here are Native Americans, who have been here the longest but are still an oppressed minority. Examples of other ethnic minorities are Asian Americans, African Americans, and Hispanic Americans.

Refugees, immigrants, and especially undocumented aliens suffer discrimination and oppression, and are characteristically outside of the social service network. The state of California has recently legally excluded undocumented aliens from eligibility for state services, such as education, health care, and income maintenance. This exclusion is being challenged in court.

C. *Social Class.* Middle-class values and norms dominate society in the United States. The upper classes, however, are generally insulated from oppression. The highest degree of oppression occurs with poverty, both urban and rural.

D. *Religion.* Christianity is the dominant religion in the United States, and societal institutions support and reflect this dominance. Minority religions are discounted and oppressed groups. Despite legally sanctioned separation of church and state, many recognized national holidays are Christian religious observances.

E. *Gender.* While women are numerically a higher percentage of the population, they are a minority in the sense that they suffer oppression and discrimination in various spheres, such as employment, housing, and the justice system (especially in terms of harassment and rape cases).

F. *Sexual Orientation.* Heterosexism is the accepted standard of sexual relationship in the United States. Homosexuals are oppressed and victimized. This oppression has been exacerbated by the spread of AIDS. Fear of AIDS in the general population has increased the stigmatization.

G. *Disabilities.* Mental or physical disability create oppressive conditions for people whose specific needs require additional, and often not available, accommodations from society. Disabled individuals are especially vulnerable to harm: as a population they are often avoided, discounted, treated as childlike, or ignored as though they were invisible. The Americans with Disabilities Act is meant to ensure equality of access to goods and services by all members of society.

H. *Appearance.* The United States has clearly defined standards for beauty and attractiveness. Appearance that differs markedly from the norm may also create oppressive conditions for the individual. Our society is designed for people within certain parameters of height and weight, and does not accommodate to gross variations from these norms. Similarly, individuals who are disfigured, either by birth or accident, may suffer reactions of avoidance or repugnance which are oppressive.

I. *Age.* Ours is a youth-oriented society. Little consideration and respect are given to the elderly, who are often discounted. With diminishing physical and mental abilities, many elderly are vulnerable to oppression and harm. Even without any diminution in functioning, however, the elderly population as a whole suffers oppression.

J. *Language and Educational Level.* Our society expects members to be literate, to have a command of the English language, to have a high school education, and to have functional skills that support functioning in the dominant society. Those who lack these skills suffer discrimination in many spheres: employment, access to education and resources, justice, housing, and other areas.

This list is far from comprehensive. It is important to remember, as noted earlier, that many people are members of more than one oppressed population. These individuals are often doubly or even triply victimized.

Oppression in the Social Work Encounter

As discussed in Chapter 3, clients bring their own self-concept, their whole identity, often affected by their experiences with vulnerability and oppression, with them to the client–worker relationship. It is recognized that these experiences will affect the relationship and that they need to be addressed in practice. Knowledge of populations other than one's own is a basic social worker responsibility, an ongoing lifelong professional endeavor. Social workers are generally open to this kind of learning and recognize its importance in their work.

It is important to remember to temper our knowledge about the specific history, needs, and problems of any oppressed population with an understanding of the effect of this on each client. Different people react and respond to oppression differently, the client's unique and specific experience must be carefully considered and understood.

Clients in need of social services often are vulnerable, at-risk, and disempowered. They are frequently members of victimized populations, and enter into the client–worker relationship with a strong history of oppression. Workers are often members of, employed by, and supportive of, the very societal institutions that oppress clients. Like members of the general population, to whom the policies and programs of the dominant society "make sense," as Reamer claims, (Reamer, 1994, p. 233) workers may be unaware of the oppressive conditions these institutions create. It is vital to competent professional practice that workers reflect carefully on these important issues.

Chapter Exercise

1. Make a list of the populations you consider oppressed within the area in which you live and work. Are there special categories or subcategories among these that are different from the categories previously listed? Describe these special groups and attempt to define/explore the reasons that they are vulnerable or oppressed.

2. Select one oppressed population that exists in reasonable numbers in your community. Can you see oppression within and among members of this population as well? How does it manifest itself in the relationships between members of the wider oppressed group?

3. Looking inward, at yourself, and make a list of the ways you, too, feel vulnerable, at-risk, disempowered, and/or oppressed. These may be drawn from the categories already listed or may be unique to you.

4. With your list before you, examine the feelings and emotions you associate with your vulnerabilities and oppressions. How do these manifest themselves in your own thinking and behavior? In your relationship with others in your group? With others in different groups?

Questions 3 and 4 are very important in understanding both yourself and others in terms of vulnerability and oppression. Devote as much time to this portion of your exercise as you need to ensure that you fully understand and accept the validity of your feelings and emotions, and their manifestations in your thoughts and behavior.

Unit I Summary

Unit I has attempted to provide you with a conceptual and contextual framework for exploring personal self-awareness. Chapter 1 presented the mission and value base of the social work profession from both a historical and an ethical perspective. Chapter 2 asked that you explore your own motivation for entering the social work profession, and that you focus on the similarity in goals and values between yourself and the profession as a whole that validate the choice you made. Acknowledging that there may be areas where your personal values and goals and those of the profession differ is also valuable in assisting you to "place" yourself within social work as a whole.

Chapter 3 explored some of the sources of imbalance inherent in the client–worker relationship, in order to assist you in examining how power, authority, and knowledge create a condition of inequality between yourself and your client. It is important for you to recognize this in considering the effect of your values, ideas, and beliefs upon clients.

Some of the groups that are oppressed in the United States were presented in Chapter 4, where divergences and differences from the established dominant "norm" create conditions of risk, vulnerability, and disempowerment.

The exercises at the end of each chapter were designed with several purposes in mind: (1) to connect your personal values, goals, and ethics to those of the profession as a whole; (2) to help you reflect on some of the broad issues involving oppression and vulnerability; and (3) to allow you opportunities to "get comfortable" with the journaling process prior to the deeper introspective work of Unit II. The unit assignment on page 47 will help you pull together all that you have learned.

Unit I Assignment

Values and Goals

The assignment asks that you define both the "outer framework" (the profession) and the "inner framework" (the person) in terms of mission, values, and goals, and explore points of convergence and divergence.

1. *The Profession.* Present your understanding of the mission and value base of the profession, as drawn from the preceding chapters and from your own observations from field and other experiences. Include populations served and special needs addressed, as well as perspectives used.

2. *The Person.* Using the work that you have done in the preceding chapters, explore the reasons that you chose the profession of social work. Define your personal values and professional goals, and illustrate how these led you to the choice you have made.

3. *Convergence and Divergences.* Review what you have written previously for profession and person. You will notice both similarities and differences. Define these similarities; thus, affirming the congruence you have found between self and profession. As noted previously, there will be areas in which your goals and values and the profession's do not fit perfectly. Acknowledge these areas.

Preparatory Notes

The Profession

The Person

Convergences and Divergences

Unit II

Exploring Self-Identity

In the next four chapters, you will be embarking on a journey toward increased self-awareness and personal identity exploration. The material that will be presented and the exercises that follow each chapter will encourage you to trace the development of your identity throughout the course of your life, and to view it within an experiential context.

As in Unit I, there are two frameworks here, an inner and an outer. The inner is your own, as your values, goals, and reasons for becoming a social worker are your own. The outer includes the groups with which you are affiliated.

The inner framework is the identity you hold personally and individually. It is the unique You. You do not share this identity with any other person, for it is a complex composed of your own genetic inheritance, life experiences, beliefs, values, and worldview.

The outer framework is a group identity you share with others in different contexts and times. For example, race, religion, social class, physical appearance, sexual orientation, and gender place you in a group with others who share those characteristics. As you will see, there are groups with which you "choose" to identify and groups to which your membership is "ascribed" by others: by the group itself or by members of other groups.

Group membership produces an awareness of "us" and "them," or of "us" and "other." This unit will assist you in defining the unique "me," as well as the group affiliated "us."

In Chapter 5, we will explore some theoretical frameworks for the development of identity. These will include comprehensive theories, as well as identity crisis theories, and specific theories which focus on racial/ethnic/cultural gender, sexual orientation, and disability identity development. In reading through the material, try to focus specifically on areas and issues that are relevant to your personal identity development.

You will find that much of this material is familiar to you, as it is included in several courses throughout the social work curriculum. It is presented here to help you explore your *own* process, rather than working to understand that of others.

In the following three chapters, we will be working toward defining personal identity: first, in Chapter 6, your identity as you perceive it today; in Chapter 7, the persons and events that you feel helped to shape your self-concept; and last, in Chapter 8, an exploration of your personal experience and understanding of "other" and "otherness."

Chapter FIVE

Theories of Identity Development

The very word *identity,* Erikson states early in his landmark book, *Identity, Youth, and Crisis* (Erikson, 1968, p. 9) "has become a term for something as unfathomable as it is all-pervasive."

Identity is a complex, multilayered concept. Our identity attests to the uniqueness and individuality of each of us and to the commonalties that exist between us. There is a sense in which we shape our own identities through experiences, learning, and choice. There is another sense in which our identities are ascribed to us by others, such as parents, teachers, friends, communities, and social institutions. Our identity is also affected by our genes and inheritance.

Identity answers the deceptively simple question: "Who am I?" The answers to the question vary with context and by whether we are seeking similarities or differences.

Extensive thought has been given by the fields of social work, psychology, sociology, and psychiatry to the manner in which self-identity develops. It is recognized that this is a process that, in the healthy person, continues throughout life. When the process of identity development is halted, the individual remains committed to a particular identity with no consideration of further or future possibilities for growth, change, and development.

This chapter does not presume to present a wide and thorough range of identity theories: entire volumes are devoted to this subject. Rather, we will explore several of the general theories, those that present a comprehensive view of identity development in many spheres and during the course of a life span. These will be exemplified by Eric Erikson's developmental stages of identity, Turner and Tajfel's social identity theory, symbolic interactionism, the ecological perspective, structural functionalism, and identity development in transpersonal theory.

There are moments when identity assumes a paramount position in the individual's thought and functioning. One of these, adolescence, is quite predictable; the others, identity crises often precipitated by changes in relationships, employment, living conditions, and status, are less predictable.

We will explore adolescent identity issues, as well as those that occur at other times.

Identity may also be considered from a more specific perspective, for our identity also includes such characteristics as race, gender, sexual orientation, disability, and moral development. These will also be introduced for your consideration.

You will be offered suggestions for further reading in each of these areas to help you expand your knowledge in those areas of greatest interest to you. You may wish to select for further exploration issues that you believe to have affected your identity development.

Comprehensive Theories of Identity Development

Personal identity is that element within us which provides a sense of continuity of self throughout the course of our lives. It includes memories of past experiences, as well as expectations and aspirations for the future. Both of these contribute to the way we perceive who and what we are in the present. We can define identity in the present, but our definition always reaches both back into the past and forward into the future.

Erik Erikson's Eight Stages of Psychosocial Development

Although Eric Erikson's (1980) work on the stages of psychosocial development is more comprehensive than our specific focus on identity formation, it is a very helpful framework within which to begin our work. Erikson views the task of identity formation as a lifelong process. In each of the eight stages of psychosocial development, a crisis occurs that must be addressed. The successful resolution of the crisis assists the individual toward self-understanding and self-definition, and the achievement of a "basic strength," which can also be perceived as a value. Failure to resolve the task of a stage of development, he states, will result in pathological development.

The stages, their psychosocial crisis, and the positive resolution follow:

1. *Infancy.* Trust vs. Mistrust. The positive resolution of this crisis develops the "basic strength" of hope.
2. *Early Childhood.* Automony vs. Shame and Doubt. The positive resolution of this crisis enables strength of will.
3. *Play Age.* Initiative vs. Guilt. The positive resolution of this crisis enables the development of a sense of purpose.
4. *School Age.* Industry vs. Inferiority. The positive resolution of this crisis permits the development of a sense of competence.
5. *Adolescence.* Identity vs. Confusion. Fidelity develops from the positive resolution of this crisis.
6. *Young Adulthood.* Intimacy vs. Isolation. The strength of love, or the capacity and desire to love, develop from the successful resolution of this crisis.

7. *Adulthood.* Generativity vs. Stagnation. The strength of care is enabled through a positive resolution of this crisis.

8. *Old Age.* Integrity vs. Despair. Successful resolution of this crisis enables wisdom.

From the perspective of identity development, the successful achievement of each of these crises, or life tasks, enables the development and fulfillment of personal values and a positive self-identity. Erikson's focus is primarily related to *individual* identity development.

Suggestions for Further Reading:
Erikson, E. (1980). *Identity and the life cycle.* New York: W.W. Norton Publishers.
Erikson, E. (1950). *Childhood and society.* New York: W.W. Norton Publishers.

Tajfel and Turner's Social Identity Theory

Henri Tajfel and John Turner focused on the development of a *social* identity in their studies of social groups and intergroup relations. The task of social identity development is crucial for each individual: a positive self-identity is essential to the development of feelings of value of self and self-worth. There is a drive toward the development of a positive self-identity and a positive comparison of self relative to others in the social environment.

Social identity is a complex composite and is based on affiliation and membership in multiple social groups. When a particular affiliation or membership is viewed in positive terms by the individual and by society, all members in that group are ascribed this positive affiliation, rather than being understood in terms of individual characteristics. Membership in a group viewed as positive establishes a positive self-image; the converse is also true.

Suggestions for Further Reading
Tajfel, H., & Robinson, W., Eds. (1997). *Social groups and identities: Developing the legacy of Henry Tajfel.* London: Butterworth Heinemann. International Series in Social Psychology.

Symbolic Interactionism

Symbolic interactionism may be defined as a perspective that "focuses attention on the processes through which persons interpret and give meaning to the objects, events, and situations that make up their social worlds" (Karp & Yoels, 1986, p. 31).

The mind of the individual understands and interprets both through language and the cognitive processes. One of the important subjects of this endeavor is personal identity, which develops from the way the individual perceives himself in relation to society and to the world around him. In this sense, symbolic interactionism views the identity in *social* terms.

We have a view of ourselves as unique individuals, but we also have two other ways of viewing ourselves: our *ideal* self, the person we wish we could be; and our *possible* self, the person we know we could be if only we tried hard enough.

We use roles to develop our personal selves, taking them on, practicing them, and integrating them as we develop throughout the life cycle. Our roles develop, change, and evolve during the process of social interaction.

One of the important concepts in symbolic interactionism is that of labeling. Labeling affects the development of self in that the person integrates into her identity the label ascribed to her by others. When the label is negative, low self-esteem and a poor self-image result (Longres, 1990).

Suggestions for Further Reading
Karp, D. A., & Yoels, W. C. (1986). *Sociology and everyday life.* Itasca, IL: F.E. Peacock Publishers.

Mead, G. H. (1934). *Mind, self, and society.* Chicago: University of Chicago Press.

The Ecological Perspective

The ecological perspective suggests that we take "a holistic view of people and environments as a unit in which neither can be fully understood except in the context of its relationship to the other. That relationship is characterized by continuous reciprocal exchanges, or transactions, in which people and environments influence, shape, and sometimes change each other" (Germain, 1991, p. 16).

Central to the ecological model is the concept of an action-oriented adaptation, a process whereby each individual strives for the best possible person-in-environment "fit" over the course of their lifetime. Adaptations may be internal (physiological, psychological), or they may be external (social, cultural). We adapt when we are confronted with life stressors, challenges that affect our growth, development, health, and/or social relationships. Major life stressors include domination, oppression, poverty, militarism, the proliferation of nuclear arms, and technological pollution of the environment (Germain, 1991, p.17–24).

Each individual also carries four important potentialities, each dependent upon the environment. These are the capacity for (1) human relatedness, (2) competence, (3) self-direction, and (4) self-esteem. While we tend to think of these as characteristics of *individuals,* Germain suggests that they are outcomes of person-environment relationships and are dependent upon the environment for their maintenance (German, 1991, p. 26–27).

It is important to consider that these four attributes appear to be free of any cultural bias, and the concepts are adaptable to a variety of circumstances.

Suggestions for Further Reading
Germain, C. B. (1991). *Human behavior in the social environment.* New York: Columbia University Press.

Structural Functionalism

Structural functionalism is built the belief that harmony and stability are possible within the social environment and that shared values, and an understanding of expectations, will support this state. These conditions offer each individual the best opportunities for achieving personal and societal goals.

However, such harmony does not always exist. When it is broken, stress, crises, and feelings of anomie occur, forcing the individual to adapt and adjust in some manner. Positive adjustments support the existing system, while negative adjustments distance the individual, causing illness and psychological disturbance.

Concepts from a structural functional perspective are drawn from Marxian theory and from the work of Emile Durkheim on anomie and are often used in social work, where they are sometimes called systems theory (Longres, 1990, p. 408).

Robert Merton, working in the 1950s, suggested that anomie is often experienced as a result of differences between opportunities and goals, and he suggests five possible adaptations: (1) conformity, (2) innovation, (3) ritualism, (4) retreatism, and (5) rebellion (Merton, 1951, p. 193–211).

Holmes and Rahe developed a Schedule of Recent Experiences to explore the kinds of life events that produce stress and, therefore, a loss in harmony and stability for the individual. The five most commonly experienced stressors were found to be (1) death of spouse, (2) divorce, (3) marital separation, (4) jail term, and (5) death of close family member (Holmes & Rahe, 1967, p. 214).

Suggestions for Further Reading

Durkheim, E. (1951). *Suicide.* New York: Free Press.

Holmes, T. H., & Rahe, R. H. (1967). The social readjustment rating scale. *Journal of Psychosomatic Research, 11*(2).

Merton, R. K. (1951). Social theory and social structure. New York: Free Press.

The Transpersonal Perspective

While Western psychology presents identity as strongly related to self and ego, and views development in terms of stages or distinct processes, the transpersonal theory suggests a more fluid, changing perspective of identity that does not necessarily progress linearly. What is included in self-identity may expand and contract during different periods and in different situations. Thus, boundaries between "me" and "other," or "not me," are flexible. "Me" can comfortably and acceptably include, not only characteristics, beliefs, actions, and behavior that are viewed as positive, but also those viewed as negative. The understanding of "me" typically includes not only the physical, intellectual, and affective self, but also the transcendental self, which embraces and incorporates all of existence at all levels. This transcendental self is perceived, therefore, as related to every "other." This allows the "me-they" dichotomy that is grounded in the physical world to become irrelevant and, therefore, resolved.

This broader conception and awareness of the relatedness of an individual to a broader entity of humanity modifies and dissolves the carefully drawn lines between which many Westerners draw their own identities.

Suggestions for Further Reading

Canda, E. R. (1991). East/West philosophical synthesis in transpersonal theory. *Journal of Sociology and Social Welfare, 18*(4), 137–52.

Cowley, A. (1993). Transpersonal social work: A theory for the 1990's. *Social Work, 38M*(5), 527–34.

McGee, E. (1984). The transpersonal perspective: Implications for the future of personal and social development. *Social Development Issues 8*(3):,158–81.

Identity Crisis

Adolescence

Perhaps with more consistency than at any other period of life, adolescence is universally accepted as a time when human beings search for and attempt to develop a self-aware identity. Adolescence is a time of pulling away from the identity of childhood, so closely related to that of parents and family groups, and movement toward a greater awareness of individuality. It is a time of rebellion and of experimentation with different beliefs, attitudes, and behavior. It is a period during which serious attention is given to the development of an ideal self and a possible self. It is also a time of seeking validation of personal identity in peers and recognition of the ascribed identity of the wider community and society.

Adolescent identity crises may be particularly stressful, difficult, prolonged, and painful for adolescents who are struggling toward an understanding and definition of themselves as racial, ethnic, or religious minorities; as gays and lesbians; or as disabled young adults. Erik Erikson's concept of the identity crises/tasks of adolescence are presented here to serve as a possible method for considering general adolescent identity development and as a framework for considering the additional identity problems faced by some adolescents.

Erikson defined the psychosocial task of adolescence as Identity vs. Confusion (Erikson, 1968). With awareness, teens must integrate their memory of the experiences and learning of childhood with their conception of their future and the meaning that this will have for them. It is a time of choices, a time of definition. For Erikson, the understanding of identity is a subjective one: identity is an awareness of the continuity of the individual from childhood, through the present, and into the future.

One may emerge from adolescence with a firm personal commitment, as *Achievers,* the product of an intense period of self-exploration decision making. One may have passed through adolescence taking a more passive role, accepting the identity that has developed and been ascribed by caregivers and others in the one's life at an earlier age. These more passive adolescents are termed *Foreclosers.* They have bypassed the struggles of the achievers by accepting others' view of them. *Diffusers* neither accept the view of others nor struggle to develop their own. They are comfortable with no firm definition of identity. Another possible group are those who are in a state of *Moratorium* on the issue of personal identity. They are struggling with career decisions, wider philosophical issues, or other needs and problems that cause them to postpone the attention needed for the development of identity for a time (Erikson, 1968).

Suggestions for Further Reading:

Arredondo, P. M. (1984). Identity themes for immigrant young adults. *Adolescence, 14*(76), 977–93.

Davidson, A. R. (1993). *Value development among Jewish adolescents: Processes of Engagement.* Unpublished doctoral dissertation, Case Western Reserve University.

Erikson, E. *(1968). Identity, youth, and crisis.* New York: Norton Publishers.

Logan, S. L. (1981). Race, identity, and black children: A developmental perspective. *Social Casework 62*(1), 47–56.

Ohannessian, C. M., Lerner, R. M., Lerner, J. V., & von Eye, A. (1994). A longitudinal study of perceived family adjustment and emotional adjustment in early adolescence. *The Journal of Early Adolescence, 14*(3), 371–90.

Phinney, J. S. (1989). Stages of ethnic identity development in minority group adolescents. *Journal of Early Adolescence, 9* (1–2), p. 34–49.

Plummer, D. L. (1995). Patterns of racial identity development of African American adolescent males and females. *Journal of Black Psychology 21*(2), 168–80.

Stevens, J. W. (1997). African American female adolescent identity development: A three dimensional perspective. *Child Welfare, 76*(1), 145–72.

Tokuno, K. A. (1986). The early adult transition and friendships: Mechanisms of support. *Adolescence 21*(83), 593–606.

Waterman, A. S. (1982). Identity development from adolescence to adulthood: An extension of theory and a review of research. *Developmental Psychology, 18*(3), 34–58.

Transitional Crisis States

Identity crisis is commonly associated with adolescence but can occur at any age. Immigration, discharge from military service, retirement where identity was strongly associated with occupational role, motherhood with an empty nest, welfare recipients with "no identity" because our culture defines identity strongly by occupation, loss of a life partner, sudden changes in physical status or abilities, and dramatic changes in life circumstances and conditions are only a few examples of situations that can create an identity crisis.

Gail Sheehy's works, *Passages* (1976) and *New Passages* (1995), introduced the concept of "passages"—transitions that occur when an earlier identity is questioned and reconsidered and a potentially new or changed one is developed. The "passage" that occurs at midlife is often manifested by an identity crisis and is a particularly difficult time, when individuals assess "where they are," and measure it against where they wanted to be. This is a time for considering radical changes and setting new goals based on the more mature self-perception that comes through life experiences and a better understanding of self.

Some consider that death, the last and greatest transition, is often accompanied by an identity crisis as well. In preparation for this transition, the dying person often takes inventory of his or her life and arrives at a final understanding and acceptance of its meaning.

Transitions, with the identity crises that generally accompany them, create tension and anxiety, and a successful passage requires introspection, self-awareness, and a willingness to make changes if necessary.

Suggestions for Further Reading
Price, R. H. (1985). Work and community. *American Journal of Community Psychology 13*(1), 1–12.
Sheehy, G. (1976). *Passages*. New York: Bantam.
Sheehy, G. (1995). *New passages: Mapping your life across time*. New York: Ballentine Books.
Weigert, A. J., & Hastings, R. (1977). Identity loss, family, and social change. *American Journal of Sociology, 82*(6),1171–85.

Racial/Ethnic/Cultural Identity Formation

Much attention has been given to identity formation based on racial affiliations. Jean Phinney's work, a suggested reading in the previous section on adolescence, presents research on minority identity formation using primarily racial characteristics (Asian American, African American, Hispanic American, and white), and much of the recent work on identity formation and development has been done in the context of race.

Whether race exists in any meaningful empirical manner or not, almost all human beings consider themselves members of a particular race; hence, the theories briefly presented here have a broad applicability. Further reading, as suggested, will greatly increase your understanding of these models.

Ethnic and cultural identity may be intimately entwined with racial identity or may exist separately.

The Cross Model of Black Racial Identity Development

Cross uses a stage model to define and describe racial identity formation:

Stage I: Pre-encounter. Internalization of dominant cultural attitudes, distance from other African Americans, move toward assimilation into white society.

Stage II: Encounter. Event forces recognition of impact of race on individual, focus on identity as member of racially oppressed group.

Stage III: Immersion/Emersion. Exploration of African American history, identity, and culture, surrounds self with symbols of blackness. Occasionally angry toward whites.

Stage IV: Internalization. Secure in African American racial identity, less defensive. Joins coalitions with other minority groups to address joint concerns, relates to whites who respect African American identity.

Stage V: Internalization/Commitment. Commitment to the African American community as a whole, able to transcend race in certain circumstances.

Fanon/Bulhan Stages of Black Identity Development

Fanon and Bulhan also use a staged model of racial identity development, but use a different structure.

Stage I: Capitulation. Identification with the dominant culture or "cultural in-betweenity," where dominated and dominating cultures experience contact, confrontation, and mutuality. (Bulhan, 1985, p. 193–94)

Stage II: Revitalization. Rejects assimilation and domination, romanticizes own culture.

Stage III: Radicalization. Active commitment to radical change in the relationship between cultures.

The Helms Model of White Racial Identity Development

Helms uses a six-stage model:

Stage I: Contact. Lack of awareness of racism and privilege, naive curiosity based on fear and stereotypes learned from others.

Stage II: Disintegration. New awareness of racism brings guilt, anger, and shame. Denial, victim-blaming, isolation from people of color and conversations about racism. Notices racist content, but confrontation is greeted with avoidance, withdrawal, dismissal, or outright hostility.

Stage III: Reintegration. Because disintegration is painful, attempt to reintegrate belief system into prevalent white racist system, anger and fear toward people of color.

Stage IV: Pseudo-Independence. Aware of importance of abandoning belief in white superiority, perhaps still unaware of personal behaviors, beliefs, and attitudes that perpetuate racism.

Stage V: Immersion/Emersion. Despite discomfort with whiteness, racism, and privilege, recognizes own whiteness, searches for a new way to be white.

Stage VI: Autonomy. Redefinition and affirmation of whiteness, able and willing to confront racism and oppression.

Although much of the work on minority racial identity development was done in reference to African Americans, it is possible to use the dominant/subordinate model with other groups as well. Sue uses a similar minority identity development model in her study of Asian American racial and cultural identity development (Sue, 1989, p. 80–86).

Identity with a particular ethnic or cultural group is often a vital part of personal identity. The degree of identification with a particular culture or national origin may be related to many aspects of assimilation/acculturation, such as generational distance from country or people of origin (first generation often identifies more closely than third or fourth), geographical distance (Mexicans may maintain closer ties than Cambodians), family of origin's identification (as Filipino or American), social relationships (friends' identifications), residence (in Little Italy or suburbia), and facility with the English language (little knowledge of English supports cultural ties with country of origin).

The establishment of a strong ethnic-cultural identity may not be possible under certain circumstances, such as adoption, history of enslavement in the United States or in the country of origin, severe persecution in country of origin, or dilution of ethnic and cultural ties due to intermarriage.

It is also important to recognize the growing number of people with varied and extremely complex racial/ethnic/cultural backgrounds, for whom historically accepted differences are meaningless. In an article entitled "Race Is Over," the *New York Times Magazine* featured photographs of a sampling of 20 children. Identities included Filipino/Italian/Russian, African American/Filipino/American Indian/French Canadian, Dominican/Russian/Jewish, African American/American Indian/Mexican, Dutch/Jamaican/Irish/African American/Russian-Jewish, Hawaiian/Chinese/Japanese, and Columbian/Scottish/Irish (Crouch, 1996, September 29, p. 170–171).

Suggestions for Further Reading

Allen, P. G. (1992). Angry women are building: Issues and struggles facing American indian women today. In M. L. Anderson & P. H. Collins (Eds.), *Race, class, and gender.* Belmont, CA: Wadsworth Publishing Co.

Betances, S. (1992). Race and the search for identity. In M. L. Anderson & P. H. Collins (Eds.), *Race, class, and gender.* Belmont, CA: Wadsworth Publishing Co.

Bulhan, H. A. (1985). *Franz Fanon and the psychology of oppression.* New York: Plenum Press, p. 193–94.

Cross, W. E. (1992). *Shades of Black: Diversity in African-American identity.* Philadelphia, PA: Temple University Press.

Crouch, S. (1996, September 29). Race is over. *New York Times Magazine,* p. 170–71.

Gushue, G. V. (1993). Cultural identity development and family assessment: An interaction model. *Counseling Psychologist, 21*(3), 487–513.

Helms, J. E. (Ed.). (1990). *Black and white racial identity: Theory, research, and practice.* Westport, CT: Greenwood Press.

Kerwin, C., Ponterotto, J. G., Jackson, B. L., & Harris, A. (1993). Racial identity in biracial children: A qualitative investigation. *Journal of Counseling Psychology, 40*(2), 221–31.

Poston, W. C. (1990). The biracial identity development model: A needed addition. *Journal of Counseling and Development, 69*(2), 152–155.

Quintana, S. M. (1994). A model of ethnic perspective-taking ability applied to Mexican-American children and youth. *International Journal of Intercultural Relations, 18*(4), 419–48.

Sue, D. W. (1989). Racial/cultural identity development among Asian Americans. *AAPA Journal,* 13(1), 80–86.

Tan, C. I. (1993). *The liberation of Asians.* Seattle, WA: Rational Island Publishers.

Gender Identity Development

It is important to distinguish carefully between biological sex and gender. While biological sex is a genetic attribute, gender is socially defined in terms of behaviors regarded by society as appropriate to one's biological sex. Thus, gender role is attributed by society and includes a much broader identity than sexual: behavior, beliefs, expectations, attitudes, values, and norms all form part of gender roles (Germain 1991, p. 250–51). Such socially determined roles can be restrictive to individuals, because they often prescribe and proscribe certain characteristics, limiting choices.

Gender identity development may be addressed from the standpoint of psychoanalytic theory, social learning theory, cognitive developmental theory and others. Bern's schema theory attempts to combine elements of both social learning and cognitive developmental theory, suggesting the child learns the particular behaviors associated with his or her own sex and, therefore, with gender (Germain, 1991, p. 252–53).

Much of the work on gender identity has been done through an exploration of moral development through the work of Piaget and, more recently, of Kohlberg and Gilligan. Kohlberg's work focused on the moral development of boys, while Gilligan developed a different pattern of moral development for girls. Kohlberg's model has been called the "rights" model and Gilligan's the "responsibility" model. There are many points of congruence between the models of moral development and male and female gender identity development.

Kohlberg's Stages of Moral Development

Level One: Pre-Conventional

Stage One: The Punishment and Obedience Orientation. "The physical consequences of an action determine its goodness or badness . . . " (Duska & Whelan, 1975, p. 45).

Stage Two: The Instrumental Relativist Orientation. Right is that which satisfies one's personal needs and very occasionally those of others.

Level Two: Conventional

Stage Three: The Interpersonal Concordance of "Good Boy–Nice Girl" Orientation. Conformity is important, and good is what is approved by others. Behavior begins to be judged by intention at this stage.

Stage Four: The Law and Order Orientation. Authority, rules, and the support of the existing social order are vital to goodness.

Level Three: Post-Conventional, Autonomous, Principled

Stage Five: The Social Contract Legalistic Orientation. Right is defined according to standards agreed on by the entire society, and there is a clear awareness that personal values and opinions may be relative. However, there is also an awareness that a change in the law is possible if necessary.

Stage Six: The Universal Ethical Principle Orientation. Individuals choose ethical principles that govern the rightness of their behavior. These are abstract, universal principles (Duska & Whelan, 1975, p. 45–47).

Gilligan's Stages of Moral Development

1. *Care of Self.* Focus on care of self to ensure survival.
2. *Judgment of Self as Selfish.* Development of a growing awareness of others and a negative judgment of oneself as selfish in caring only about personal survival and needs.
3. *Responsibility for Others.* Heightened perception of the interconnectedness of self and others, which leads to a sense of responsibility for others.

4. *Fusion of Responsibility with Maternal Morality.* Greater sense of responsibility causes concern for others above self, especially those who are dependent and needy. Good is caring for others.

5. *Awareness of Exclusion of Self.* Caring for others above self introduces a disequilibrium in relationships. There is a confusion between self-sacrifice and needs of self.

6. *Focus on Dynamics in Relationships.* Conflict is resolved through a reconsideration of the relationship between self and "other." Care becomes a self-chosen principle that recognizes the interdependence of all people (Gilligan, 1982).

Suggestions for Further Reading

Duska, R., & Whelan, M. (1975). *Moral development: A guide to Piaget and Kohlberg.* New York: Paulist Press.

Gilligan, C. (1982). *In a different voice.* Cambridge, MA: Harvard University Press.

Gilligan, C. (1982). New maps of development: new visions of maturity. *American Journal of Orthopsychiatry, 52*(2),199–212.

Rhodes, M. L. (1985). Gilligan's theory of moral development as applied to social work. *Social Work, 30*(2), 101–5.

Reimer, M. S. (1983). Gender differences in moral judgment: The state of the art. *Smith College Studies in Social Work, 54*(1), 1–12.

Gay and Lesbian Identity Development

While sexual orientation may become a central identity issue at any time, adolescence is generally the period during which individuals become aware of sexual orientation. Moses and Hawkins define sexual orientation as referring to three aspects of identity: (1) physical (past and present preference in sexual partners); (2) affectional (past and present gender preference in primary emotional relationships); and (3) fantasy (past and present preferences in partners in sexual fantasy). They note that some people have no preference; others have preferences, but these may not match in all three areas (Moses & Hawkins, 1982).

For teenagers who recognize a same-sex orientation, there is often a period of confusion and conflict, and "coming out" may be a painful and difficult process. Moses and Hawkins identify four steps in the process: (1) self-labeling as a gay person; (2) coming out to others; (3) coming out to nongay persons; and (4) going public (Moses & Hawkins, 1982).

Suggestions for Further Reading

Cox, S., & Gallois, C. (1996). Gay and lesbian identity development: A social identity perspective. *Journal of Homosexuality, 30*(4), 1–30.

Morrow, D. S. (1996). Coming-out issues for adult lesbians: A group intervention. *Social Work, 41*(6), 647–56.

Moses, A. E., & Hawkins, R. O. (1982). *Counseling lesbian women and gay men: A life-issues approach.* St. Louis, MO: Mosby Publishers.

Nichols, M., & Leiblum, S. R. (1986). Lesbianism as a personal identity and social role: A model. *Affilia Journal of Women and Social Work, 1*(1), 48–59.

Disabled Person Identity Development

Persons with disability are often similar only in being differently abled than the general population: they are an otherwise heterogeneous group. Their disability may affect their physical or mental functioning. However, it also always affects their social functioning, as the disability creates a social role identity.

Germain views disability as a life stressor. As such, coping mechanisms are put in place by the individual. These may be either adaptive or maladaptive (Germain, 1991).

Exploring disability from the perspective of equity theory, Weinberg focused on persons who were orthopedically disabled. She found that these persons felt that able-bodied persons violated their personal rights by staring at them, asking personal and intrusive questions, offering unasked-for assistance, and humiliating them publicly. The disabled individuals responded to this behavior with anger, dissatisfaction, and hostility. Most of the people studied accommodated in a passive manner, and few responded assertively. Thus, the inequity remained unchanged, while the individual adapted to it by learning to put up with it or learning to accept it (Weinberg, 1983, p. 365–69).

A perhaps more positive approach is Wolfensberger's social role valorization theory, which suggests that it is possible to "normalize" a disabled person by enabling and supporting the development of positive social roles. Such roles become incorporated into the public image of the person and the disability so that a positive association, rather than a negative one, is made. Thus, the disabled person is able to develop self-esteem and a positive personal identity (Thomas & Wolfenseberger, 1982, p. 356–58).

Suggestions for Further Reading

Steer, M. (1989). A powerful concept for disability policy and service provision. *Australian Social Work, 42*(1), 43–47.

Thomas, S., & Wolfensberger, W. (1982). The importance of social imagery in interpreting societally devalued people to the public. *Rehabilitation Literature, 43*(11–12), 356–58.

Weinberg, N. (1983). Social equity and the physically disabled. *Social Work, 28,* 365–69.

Chapter Exercise

This chapter has explored theories of identity development from a variety of perspectives and suggested further readings to help you gain a deeper knowledge. Select and read any two of the suggested readings that you feel will enhance your understanding of *your own* identity development.

Summarize what you have learned from each.

Chapter SIX

Exploring and Affirming Your Personal Identity

In the preceding chapters, we explored some of the characteristics of client populations for whom our profession has a special responsibility, examined our own feelings and thoughts about our personal status in this regard, and examined some theories of identity development. Each of us has also selected one or more theories to work with which seem to exemplify the way we understand identity development.

Here, we will begin a deeper exploration of our own identity, recognizing that a thorough understanding of ourselves is necessary to our work with others. In our work, we will attempt to reach an understanding and defining of "self" and then explore what "self" believes and feels about "other."

It is important to acknowledge that the exploration on which we are embarking will not always be easy nor pleasant. There will be exhilarating moments of self-affirmation and self-validation, and painful moments of acknowledgment that, through circumstances both within and without ourselves, we are not the people that we would like ourselves to be or that we have always believed ourselves to be.

We will begin this process by examining our values, worldview, interests, and personal characteristics. Then, we will move to an exploration and definition of the groups, populations, or categories with which we identify. Together, these elements will enable us to understand how we view our own identity today. Because identity development is a lifelong process, it is important to recognize that the picture we draw today may change, develop, and refine itself as it is affected by future events and experiences. The theories of identity development presented in the last chapter can provide a useful framework for self-assessment.

Individual Identity

Personal Values and Beliefs

One of the basic ways we define ourselves as individuals is through our personal values and beliefs. We perceive ourselves as, for example, an honest person, a fair person, a trustworthy person, a person of faith, etc.

As you begin to look inward, you will immediately become aware that there is a difference between the "ideal" person you want to be and the "real" person that you are. It is a part of the human condition—unless you are a saint or a hero and, therefore, in a special category—to have this pull between the exigencies of life within which the "real" person must live and the clarity and purity of the vision of the "ideal" person. This pull is what Longres is referring to with the definitions of ideal self and possible self in the material presented at the beginning of Chapter 5.

This division between "real" and "ideal" is by no means complete; rather, there is a great amount of overlap between the two visions of self we each possess. If we were to attempt to draw ourselves along a continuum in this regard, it might look something like this:

————————————I————————————————————I—————————

The "me" that sometimes does things not in consonance with my personal values, affected by a conflict between values, desires, needs, or expediency.	The "me" that functions smoothly in everyday life with little or no awareness between values.	The "me" that always lives in full accordance with my personal values no matter what the circumstances.

Our task is to fill in each of these sections: to understand the circumstances, conditions, and terms that cause us to diverge from our personal values, beliefs, and ideals; to recognize and affirm the person we are in our everyday lives; and to grasp the ideal person we would like to always be, living always in accord with our highest values.

One of the first and perhaps clearest elucidations of values is found in classical Greek thought in the writings of Aristotle. Aristotle believed that values, as traits of character, were *learned*. We learn to be honest, fair, and consider others in the process of our training and education. Thus, our experiences in early childhood, at home, at school, and in our communities will help to determine the traits of character we develop and the values we espouse. We will be exploring the influence of others on our self-identity in greater depth in Chapter 7.

Sisela Bok's (1989) book, *Lying: Moral Choice in Public Life,* can be useful in addressing these matters of values and choices. Bok suggests that most people would agree that lying is wrong. Honesty, for most of us, falls in that middle place along the continuum of behavior. However, Bok explores the circumstances under which it might be acceptable to lie and finds that these can include: to save a life; to ensure national security; and in wartime.

There are other circumstances that she suggests we might consider, and she takes the position that some of these are individually determined. For example, if your friend is about to go out on a date and asks you if her dress is nice, and you don't like it, would you tell her the truth or lie to save hurt feelings? These kinds of "everyday" lies may seem to have little moral import, yet if living in accordance with your values and your ideal sense of self is important to you, you may find these kinds of lies significant value issues.

Another example may be found in the value of peace and nonviolence taken by some religious groups, such as the Amish. Espousing the personal value of life, the Amish do not fight in wars, even if these wars are for self-defense. It is preferable to lose one's own happiness, freedom, or even life, according to these values, than to take the life of another.

Most of us do find that there are circumstances that sometimes place us toward the left side of the value continuum. Knowing what these circumstances are is of vital import to the process of self-awareness.

Beliefs may be either individual, and developed from personal thought and experiences, or communal, developed through group affiliation and shared with others. Membership in a temple, mosque, church, or synagogue are examples of communal expressions of belief. We will be exploring group affiliations later in this chapter. However, it is also important to recognize that beliefs, though held in common, may still manifest and lead to action in a way that is personal and individual.

Personal Worldview

Often but not always closely associated with personal values and beliefs is one's personal worldview. What, for example, is your view of the nature of existence, the purpose of human life, why and how change occurs? Do you value the traditions and culture of the past and its influence on your daily life, or are you focused on the here-and-now? Do you feel that life must be enjoyed moment by moment, or are there times when you may sacrifice for the future?

Our worldview includes a complex of issues that "locate" us in the world. They are as broad as our understanding of the cosmos or as narrow as our understanding of a specific conversation.

To assist you in thinking through your personal worldview, several areas you might want to explore are described below. This is by no means considered an exhaustive list. Feel free to add your own ideas.

Time Orientation   Some of us find that living in the moment enables us to enjoy each day and experience life for itself while it is occurring. If you see yourself this way, you are *present*-oriented. You may feel very connected to the past and reference present events to memories, recollections, or family history, viewing your present experiences in a historical context. If you do, your time orientation is to the *past*. On the other hand, you may relate present events to the future and live and plan for a future time, such as "when I graduate," "when I have children," or "when I get old." If so, you are *future*-oriented.

Place or "Community" Orientation   Locating yourself in space provides another dimension of orientation. Do you see yourself as oriented primarily within your *neighborhood,* your *community,* your *city* or *town, state,* or within the *nation* as a whole? You may draw your space orientation as widely as you like—to the *continent,* the *planet,* or even the *galaxy.*

Locus of Control   Do you control events in your life and shape your life through your actions, thoughts, and beliefs? Do you believe that you are responsible for yourself? If so, your locus of control is *internal.* If you believe that your life is not in your personal control, because it is directed by a supernatural being, fate, predestination, another person or group of persons, or because you believe that events are random and you individually have no control over them, your locus of control is *external.*

Nature and the Environment   Do you believe that nature is to be honored and cared for, enjoyed but not disturbed, or that you are a part of nature as nature is a part of you? If so, your orientation is toward *respecting* it. You might instead believe that nature is provided for you to use to improve your life circumstances and those of humanity as a whole. If so, your orientation is toward *harnessing* it.

Decision Making   When arriving at a decision, do you determine what you wish to achieve or accomplish and focus primarily on the goal? If so, your decision making is determined by *ends* that you choose. If you focus instead on the methods you will use, or on how your actions will impact others, you are *means*-oriented.

Age Orientation   While your age orientation may be influenced by your chronological age, age orientation refers to the part of the lifespan you value the most. We tend to be a youth-oriented society, and we therefore place the greatest value on youth. However, you may personally value *childhood, youth, maturity,* or *old age.* Each age orientation is associated with certain values. Old age, for example, is associated with wisdom and experience, childhood with potential, and maturity with achievement and power.

Family   Much public attention has been focused in recent years on the definitions of family, and your definition is a basic part of your worldview. Do you define family as *nuclear* only? Or do you include *extended* family members? Do families have to be *biologically related?* Do you prefer a *non-biologically based* definition such as that suggested in Chapter 6, as a group of people sharing space who care for one another and contribute to the overall good of the group?

Gender   Do you tend to look at the world from a perspective you believe you share with others of your gender? Or do you tend to see the world through the eyes of the opposite gender? You may have a *male* or *female* orientation. Gender-based orientations are usually but not necessarily based on biological sex. There is also the possibility of a *nongender-based* orientation.

Interpersonal Orientation This concept explores the way in which you see yourself in relation to others. Do you view yourself as a self-determined, autonomous person, accountable primarily to yourself for your actions? You may then be *individually centered.* You may instead be *group-centered,* viewing yourself primarily as a member of a group (family, community, organization), with individual needs and identity less important than the well-being of the group as a whole.

Role of Ritual and Tradition Most of us have certain rituals and traditions that we observe. These are often associated with life-cycle events, such as marriage, birth, death, and religious and secular maturity, but may also be "the way we have always done things" for seasonal events such as Thanksgiving and Fourth of July. Are these rituals and traditions *central* to the way you live, or relatively *unimportant?* You may also find them completely *irrelevant.*

Personal Interests and Abilities

A part of our identity also includes our personal interests and abilities. If our interests and abilities match well, we find ourselves successful and fulfilled in pursuing them. If they do not, the stress engendered may disturb our sense of personal identity.

For this reason, many people choose interests that are consonant to their abilities. If you are athletic, you may enjoy playing tennis, running a marathon, or joining a volleyball league. If you are musical, you may be interested in singing in a choral group, playing in a community orchestra, or gathering with friends for an evening of music. If you are adept at working with computers, you may join Internet chat groups, design Websites for friends, or explore designing innovative software.

Often, it is possible to combine interests, abilities, and employment, and many find this arrangement fulfilling and gratifying. The athlete can turn professional, coach, or teach high school sports. The musician can become a composer, play clarinet, or lead a chorus. The computer expert can find almost unlimited employment opportunities in our technological society.

If you are interested in something but don't (objectively or subjectively) believe that you have the ability to become directly involved, you can still follow your interest by learning about it, watching it, or following related paths. A person interested in athletics can find fulfillment in being a spectator, especially in supporting a particular team. He or she can become a sports announcer, sports columnist, designer of sports equipment, agent, or venue manager.

It is important to consider your personal interests and abilities from as broad a perspective as possible. It is good to have a wide range of interests and to explore your abilities in many areas: physical, intellectual, and spiritual.

The awareness of the breadth of your interests can also help you in working with clients. Often, expanding interests and possibilities is a vital part of work with social work's traditional populations.

Personal Characteristics

An important part of self-identity is how we view our bodies, minds, personalities, and spiritual natures. Perhaps more so than our values, beliefs, worldview, interests, or abilities, our feelings about the way we look, our mental ability, and our awareness of our spiritual being is affected by our milieu.

Our perception of our attractiveness and intelligence, our judgment of ourselves, the value placed on our interests and abilities, and our feelings about our identity are often relative to the surroundings in which we find ourselves. If our friends are all athletes and we are an overweight couch potato, we may judge ourselves more harshly relative to them. If we are intelligent and are achieving A's in a community college, we may take a special pride in our accomplishment relative to that of our less-gifted classmates.

Much has been written on the subject of body image and its contribution to self-identity. Our view of ourselves as attractive or unattractive, fat or thin, light or dark skinned, blue or brown eyed, tall or short, "different" from others or similar, and the degree of importance we attribute to these physical characteristics is, at least in part, a reflection of the extreme value our society places on physical beauty.

Many of us are overly concerned with what we perceive to be our negative physical characteristics. Often, our perceptions are distorted by things we have been told by others or by life experiences we (possibly mistakenly) attribute to negative physical characteristics. We tend to be our own harshest judges, and the deaths of anorexic and bulimic young women sadly attest to both distorted perceptions and the value and importance our society places on physical attractiveness.

How we perceive our intelligence, or mental ability, also has a strong effect on our self-identity. Being labeled as learning disabled, dyslexic, or mentally disabled may create a negative self-image that persists for life and also affects our perception of other, not necessarily related, characteristics, such as the ability to concentrate, manual dexterity, and physical attractiveness. If we believe, or are told, that we are very intelligent, we may develop unusually high and demanding expectations of ourselves, thus dooming ourselves to potential failure. Being the class genius carries issues that differ from those of being the class dummy, but both extremes can have a strong impact on the life choices that we make.

We also have a perception of ourselves as feeling, or emotional, beings. We have beliefs and feelings about the way we see ourselves with other people, about what we may refer to as our personalities. We see ourselves as quiet, shy, stubborn, outgoing, persistent, compliant, argumentative, curious, nosey, or friendly. We analyze ourselves with Myers-Briggs scales and determine whether we are introverts or extroverts, intellectual or emotional, rational or intuitive. We associate positive and negative feelings with these personality characteristics as well, valuing some and disliking or being embarrassed of others.

Spirituality, faith, and religion also have a strong impact on identity. Spirituality, although it is understood and experienced individually, is a quality of all human beings. However, different people have different degrees of spiritual *awareness* and value spirituality differently. Faith is the personal belief system an individual uses to reach the transcendent. Faith may or may not include a belief in God. When a group of people share the same belief system and practice it in communal form, we say that they are sharing a religion. Because religion is experienced communally, it is considered a group affiliation rather than a personal characteristic.

Ascribed, Prescribed, and Self-Selected Identity

Group or population membership may be selected by the individual as a matter of free choice. We recognize, however, that rarely, if ever, are our choices of identity truly "free." We are all subject to various kinds of constraints: these may be physical, mental/psychological, legal, or social. We may be constrained by where we live, how we have been raised, and what we have been taught. In spite of this, we have certain freedoms in choosing some individual characteristics and group affiliations, and less or none in choosing others.

For example, we generally have little choice about gender: it is determined at birth and can be changed only through a major surgical and psychological undertaking. We have no choice about our age: as long as we remain alive, the years proceed, one after the other. We may have no choice about our sexual orientation, our refugee or immigrant status, or about handicapping conditions.

There are other group affiliations about which we may have choices under certain conditions. While race is generally not something we believe we have much choice about, those with mixed racial backgrounds may be able to choose the group with whom they will identify. A first-generation immigrant has little choice about ethnicity; his fourth generation descendant, however, may or may not choose to identify with his great-grandparents' ethnicity. Similarly, those with mixed ethnic backgrounds who are, for example, one-eighth African American, one-eighth Polish, one-fourth Mexican, and one-half Filipino have more of a choice in deciding with which group, if any, to identify.

Changes in class, education, religion, status, and regions of the country with which one identifies also may offer opportunities for personal choices. It is easy to move across group lines between generations or even within one's own life span. If you are born in Alabama but have lived for 15 years in Missouri and plan to remain there, where do you say that you are from? If you were born in Oklahoma but your family moved to California when you were two, how do you view your relationship to Oklahoma?

If you have lived and worked in New York but retire to Florida, with which area of the country do you identify? Chances are the answer will depend on who you are with, what your needs are, and why the issue is being raised.

If you're reminiscing about old times with old friends, you may be from New York; if you're applying for senior citizen's housing, you may be from Florida.

Membership in groups is also often relative to the context. Anyone who has traveled overseas has noticed the feeling of "we-ness" that occurs when one finds someone else from the United States. We feel an immediate sense of relationship and kinship with that person. We also tend to feel that his or her actions, in this foreign land, will be a reflection on the whole of the United States.

We can draw the affiliation circle narrower and narrower: to our state, our city or town, our neighborhood, our block. Each time we narrow the circle, we exclude groups of people.

These kinds of choices enable us to self-select certain aspects of our identity. However, there are also powerful forces outside of ourselves that ascribe to us membership in certain groups and mandate exclusion from others. Often, members of a group define membership or exclusion for others. A light-skinned Hispanic may not be defined by other Hispanics as Hispanic and may be excluded from group membership. If your accent is Southern, 50 years in Boston will not make Bostonians regard you as a New Englander.

Often, it is the dominant members of a particular group, or members of the dominant societal group, that determine group membership for others. Thus, no matter how strongly you may wish to affiliate with a certain group or believe that you are "entitled" to be a member of it, you may be excluded by other members of that group. This exclusion can be difficult and painful, and lead to feelings of hostility, anger, and oppression.

We repeat this process over and over in many contexts and situations, defining and redefining our identities as parts of certain groups and not as parts of others. This creates a sensation of both inclusion and exclusion. We draw strength from "us"; we become aware of differences from "other."

The groups with which we affiliate, and how we place ourselves within them, often vary not only by context but by our own choices and perceptions. Most allow for very broad categorizations, such as "person with disability," to very narrow ones, such as "chronic schizophrenic." As you read over the following potential group affiliations, reflect on the possible subcategories in each and the overlap between group affiliations as well.

There are an infinite number of potential groups with which we can affiliate. The following list presents some of the most common:

1. *Gender.* As noted earlier, there is little choice about this affiliation.

2. *Age Group.* This seems a simple affiliation, but it may become complex due to categories within categories which we use to define age. Seniors, for example, may be 55, 62, or 65, depending on the circumstances. Middle age often begins and ends with blurred age delineations also. Generational age groups with such labels as the "silents," the "boomers," and "generation X" leave some people uncomfortable with the generalizations and leave others, who seem a distinct group, nameless (and voiceless). We may "act our age," or not. We may choose to identify with a younger or older group.

3. *Race.* The visibility of racial differences reinforces the social differences between different racial groups and heightens racial consciousness (Park, 1950). This visibility often encourages stereotyping,

prejudice, and discrimination. It obscures the incompatibility between genetics and the concept of racial groups.

The term race itself carries "ambiguous and often contradictory meanings," which make it no longer very useful (Hraba, 1994, pg. 30). You may find it preferable as a professional to use the term ethnicity as inclusive of what are commonly regarded as racial groups.

Discover Magazine's special issue on "the Science of Race" has been followed by a multitude of other scientific and political explorations of the concept of race, all attempting to address this issue that seems to persist in its pervasive importance within our culture. Despite scientific evidence that there is no such thing as "race" as we know it, we "human beings are visual animals," so the concept of race continues to be acknowledged (Hoffman, 1994).

Mixed racial/ethnic/cultural heritage is common in the United States. Often, this allows a measure of individual choice in racial affiliation.

4. *Ethnicity.* Ethnic groups are self-conscious groups of people who, on the basis of a common origin or a separate subculture, maintain a distinction between themselves and others" (Hraba, 1994, p. 29).

   Some sociologists regard ethnicity in terms of majority and minority groups only, while others regard all groups, whether "racial" or "ethnic," as ethnic groups (Hraba, 1994, p. 30).

5. *Class.* When affiliations are discussed in a public forum, such as a classroom or discussion group, the levels of discomfort appear greater during discussions of class than with any other type of affiliation. "Socioeconomic," that term we associate with class, is vastly complex and suggests a number of different things, such as income, educational level, culture, and ethnicity.

   Nonetheless, Langston's (1992) article on class begins with a list we can easily recognize and which points to the existence of *something* that might be labeled as class differences: "I. Magnin, Nordstrom, The Bon, Sears, Penney's, K-Mart, Goodwill, Salvation Army."

   Part of our discomfort with the whole notion of class comes from our national ideals and perceptions—we don't want to recognize that we have such a thing as class in our ideally egalitarian society. There is another aspect to our discomfort: do we belong to the class of our parents, to the class determined by our present economic status, to the class we aspire to join, to our cultural and educational class, or to our economic class?

6. *Religious Affiliation.* As noted earlier, religion is a communal expression of faith. As such, it involves groups of people who often form strong social and cultural ties, as well as religious ones. Each religion has within itself many groupings and subgroupings, and people may identify broadly, such as "Christian," specifically, such as "Lutheran Church, Missouri Synod," as a student recently did, or anywhere along this broad continuum.

7. *Sexual Orientation.* While sexual orientation is also a personal characteristic, people tend to group themselves socially in this manner as well, forming distinct and clearly visible clusters in society. More recently, sexual orientation has taken on a cultural connotation, and we speak of the "heterosexual culture," the "homosexual culture," and the "transsexual culture," for example, as distinct from each other.

8. *Refugee, Immigrant, Undocumented Alien Status.* Not the legal status only, but also the country of origin, separates those newly arrived in the United States from each other, and from other groups in society. Refugees, immigrants, and undocumented aliens are also members of recognizable ethnic groups, and their status often reflects the status of the entire group in our society.

9. *Education.* Education may be considered separately, but it may also be grouped under "class," or "socioeconomic class." Generally, people tend to affiliate and socialize with others of similar educational levels, and status is accorded by educational level as well.

10. *Handicapping Conditions.* The Americans with Disabilities Act creates a broad category of people with disabilities without regard to kind or degree. However, as with other affiliations and groupings, there are categories within categories here as well, beginning with the first broad division between mental, emotional, and physical disability and proceeding along an ever-narrowing continuum.

11. *Region or Section of Country.* At first glance, this affiliation or grouping might seem of minor importance. However, to many, their city, area, state, or region of the country is of primary importance in the way they view themselves.

Chapter Exercise

The focus of this chapter has been a consideration of the personal, unique, and individual characteristics of your own identity. You can define yourself personally using the categories in the chapter as your guide. Remember, this chapter includes not only personal characteristics, but also those which you share with other members of a group, such as race, gender, or age.

The objective is to attempt to define *yourself*. There is a deliberate looseness, or vagueness, in the following outline which is meant to encourage you to "fill in the blanks," to expand some categories and to contract others as needed.

1. Using the guide provided, define your worldview. Allow yourself time to work on this: you may not have consciously considered some of these categories before, though you live them daily!

Worldview

2. Define some of the values and beliefs that you hold, and attempt to put these in hierarchical order.

Values and Beliefs Hierarchy

3. Prepare two lists: one of your interests and one of your abilities. To help you think of these, review the things you have enjoyed doing during the past year and the things you have done well. After you have prepared the lists, compare them, and evaluate how and where they complement each other.

Interests and Abilities

4. Take a deep breath! This task is often difficult. Remember to be kind to yourself, and try not to judge yourself too harshly.

Physical Characteristics

Mental Characteristics

Personality Characteristics

Spiritual Characteristics (Take care to remain
on an *individual, personal* plane—on the level of faith
and/or spirituality. Religion is a *group* affiliation.)

5. Define yourself in each of these group or population categories. You may find it necessary to select categories both by ascription and self-identification.

Gender

Age Group

Race

Ethnicity

Class

Religious Affiliation

Sexual Orientation

Refugee, Immigrant, Undocumented Alien Status

Education

Handicapping Conditions

Region or Section of Country

Other Affiliation (any group with which you affiliate
that is not included in the categories previously listed)

You have now described a composite of your own identity as you understand it. Allow yourself some time to reflect on what you have written during this exercise, and reorganize and refine it as needed. This exercise is the most important building block of your self-awareness in working professionally and competently with others.

Use the space provided to express any thoughts and feelings engendered as you completed this exercise.

Chapter SEVEN

Recognizing the Influence of Others on Your Personal Identity Development

As you worked through the exercises of Chapter 6, you may have noticed, in thinking about your values and beliefs, interests, physical characteristics, memberships and affiliations, and other categories of personal identity, that most of these seemed to be related to the world around you. This world, in a true person-in-environment manner, both affects you and is affected by your presence.

As you developed and matured in childhood and adolescence and moved outward from yourself, you encountered first your family group and then the broader world of school, neighborhood, and community. As you moved out into the work world, employers and colleagues, as well as adult friends, influenced your identity.

The world of the very young child is held firmly within the family group. As the child enters school, peers and teachers become strong influential factors in development and self-identity. Church, synagogue, mosque, or temple; community groups; Scouts; Boy's and Girl's Clubs; and any other groups with which the family is affiliated affect personal identity as well. As the child grows, contacts with outsiders increase, and there is a higher degree of self-selection in activities, friends, and organization membership.

These formative years of childhood and adolescence have a strong impact on our self-perception: an effect that, for most of us, remains with us for life. Many emerge from this process with a positive self-image and a strong concept of personal identity. Others emerge with self-hatred and low self-esteem. Most of us emerge somewhere in the middle—with some negative and some positive feelings about ourselves.

In general, vulnerability, powerlessness, and oppression, in and of themselves, shift the self-image balance toward the negative. Clients often carry this negative self-image with them to the professional encounter, and as we have noted in Unit I, it is important for the social worker to recognize the many possible ways this may occur within the client–worker relationship.

If the worker is also a member of a minority or an oppressed group, this, too, becomes a part of the client–worker experience.

It is not necessary, however, to be a member of an oppressed group to carry self-hatred and low self-esteem. Many of our feelings about who we are—both positive and negative—come from our experiences during our formative years.

The Family

Definitions of family vary in many ways. In the broadest sense, we can say that a family is a group of individuals sharing a common living space, who are interdependent and share the responsibility for carrying out the various functions necessary to meet the needs of each member and the good of the whole.

While the U.S. Census Bureau, and many social scientists, still hold to the relationship necessity in its definition of family as by blood, marriage, or adoption (U.S. Bureau of the Census, 1987), others, such as Karen Lindsay, suggest that family can consist of any group of individuals who share a history, love each other, and have lived together during major portions of their lives (Lindsay, 1981).

One of the most important functions of family is the care and nurturance of the children in the family group. Nurturance means the provision not only of physical needs, but of intellectual, emotional, and spiritual ones as well.

In thinking about the various areas of identity discussed in Chapter 6, and of your own identity as you defined it in the chapter exercise, you will note that there are certain parts of your identity that you share in common with other members of your family. Some of these are selected (generally by the older members of the group), and some are ascribed. Identity aspects that may be selected, such as religious affiliation, ethnicity, values, and worldviews, may be taught by older members to younger members, thus passing on an identity or affiliation from one generation to the next.

There may be other aspects of your identity that you share with some family members but not with others, such as gender, status (child, teen, adult, powerful, weak), physical appearance, interests and abilities, or personality traits.

There are also aspects of identity that belong to you alone. The areas in which you stand alone among family members are generally those that leave you most vulnerable to the approval or disapproval of other members, especially those in a position of greater power. This leads potentially to the development of positive or negative feelings about these parts of your identity.

Identity differences among family members may become more pronounced as the younger members grow and are influenced by the world outside of the immediate family circle. The family, and individual members within it, may receive these differences with positive acceptance, with indifference, or with varying degrees of negativity. Each member is affected, and affects, differences between and among themselves as family members.

The family, *as a whole,* is also affected in terms of identity by its relationship to the extended family, neighborhood, and community. A family may be identified by others as the "troublemakers" (those with the kids who are always in trouble and the parents who fight), as the "irresponsible" ones (those who don't keep their yards neat and clean and contribute to the general quality of community life), the "self-righteous" ones (those who always think their way of doing things is the only right way), the "poor" ones (those who never seem to earn enough to make ends meet), and above all, the "different" ones, the "outsiders," for any number of reasons, such as appearance, religion, language, customs, or sexual orientation.

Such ascription of difference by others will affect the self-image of the family as a whole and also that of each member. It can strengthen the bonds between members and encourage solidarity, or it can weaken them, as members seek to escape the difference labels and the negativity that is usually associated with these.

Although you are now a mature adult, your family's influence on the development of your identity continues. A very relevant example: you have chosen to assume a new aspect of identity—that of a social work professional. Your family's perception of this choice can affect your identification with the profession as a whole, your functioning within it, and many other areas of your identity and self-image, as well as your place within your family circle.

Understanding the effect and influence of your family and individual members within it on the development of your identity and on your feelings about it, is a vital part of increasing self-awareness.

The Extended Family Group

In addition to the members of an individual's own household, other family members also influence identity development. In some cases, grandparents, aunts, uncles, and cousins are a part of the household and are considered part of the "family" in its inclusive definition. However, in our mobile society, extended family members are often separated by great distances, and the degree of contact and influence vary markedly.

If you had to make choices about ethnicity, culture, religion, and other categories in Chapter 6, you may have noticed that some of these choices were influenced by your relationship with, and feelings about, extended family members. Your ethnic background, for example, may be one-fourth Turkish and three-fourth Iranian, yet your Turkish grandmother took care of you, and you loved her, so you "choose" Turkish ethnicity over Iranian. It is not necessary that you decide that there is an inherent higher value, somehow, to being Turkish: all that is necessary is that you loved your grandmother.

In many cases, grandparents play an especially important part in the development of identity, serving as teachers of morals, values, religious beliefs, and customs, and acting as role models and allies. There is often a strong alliance between grandparents and grandchildren, both of whom understand and share a relationship with the parent. Children can identify with a grandparent's appearance, beliefs, personality traits, interests, and abilities in the same way that they identify with those of parents.

Aunts, uncles, cousins of all degrees, stepparents, even "honorary" family members often also have a strong impact on self-perception, identification, and self-image.

The School and Peer Group

As children enter school and relate to peers in the neighborhood, the circle of those whose influence affect their identity development widens.

Teachers, as figures of power and authority, have a strong impact on a child's self-perception. Their personal values, interests, affiliations, biases, and prejudices, as well as their own self-images affect the growth and development of the children whose lives they touch in many ways other than the "three Rs." As teachers are presumed to have professional expertise and objectivity, parents are often strongly influenced by a teacher's perception of their child's personality, capacity, and behavior.

As Jencks (1972) has noted, it is at school that many children first begin to receive messages of what they can and cannot do as adults. Overt sex stereotyping in the classroom is decreasing, but many adults have learned expected role behaviors and career choices in school (Levy, 1974).

Studies have shown that children tend to perform in the classroom in a way that meets the teacher's expectations. If a teacher expected you to be disruptive, chances are strong that you became so. If a teacher expected you to get 100 percent on every spelling test, chances are that you did. If a teacher expected you to be noisy, neat, quiet, sloppy, or punctual, you probably were. You learned what was expected—expected behavior was reinforced, unexpected behavior ignored. You were "behaviorally conditioned"—we all were—by teachers' perceptions and expectations. Studies of the effects of gender differences on teacher expectations and resultant student behavior and performance have further validated the strong effect teacher's attitudes and responses have on student's self-images and performance.

Additionally, the influence of friends, schoolmates, clubmates, and neighborhood playmates on self-perception and identity increase with each year of growth, reaching the highest level of influence during adolescence. All groups of children have subgroupings within them, and there is a ranking of power and status within these subgroupings. Acceptance in a high-status group will contribute strongly to the development of a positive self-image, while rejection, isolation, and scapegoating will negatively affect identity development.

As we have seen in Chapter 5, adolescence is a particularly difficult and vulnerable time of development, where self-image is strongly associated with peers, and the evaluation of peers in a position of power can often have wide-ranging effects.

Adolescence is also a time of pulling away from family, of experimentation, and of the struggle to find one's own space and place in the world. Still a part of the family but preparing to move out and away, the difficult times of adolescence present identity tasks of special poignancy.

The Community

A part of self-identity is grounded in community, both in terms of affiliation and experiences. Generally, people are involved with several different kinds of communities, each of which may have a strong effect on identity perception.

1. *Locational.* Locational communities occur within neighborhoods or residences. Attachment and experience with these kinds of communities is based both on place and people.

2. *Identificational.* These communities are based on a shared identity rather than a particular place. Examples of these kinds of communities include religious, ethnic, racial, social class, and sexual orientation. Identificational communities generally share a common culture.

3. *Shared Interest.* Shared interest communities include occupational groups, such as scientists, teachers, and builders, each of whom share common interests.

Because of the pattern of segregation in the United States, locational communities are often identificational communities (Longres, 1990).

A positive identification with the community can contribute strongly to the development of a healthy self-image and high self-esteem. Conversely, negative experiences and associations, exclusion, ridicule, or ostracism will have a strong and unhealthy influence. Because of the association between locational and identificational communities, families who live in one area but identify or are identified as members of another community may experience difficulties that affect children's identity development.

The importance of the role of community, the complex and interwoven network of relationships within which optimal growth and development for children occur, is supported by the popularity of Hillary Rodham Clinton's bestselling *It Takes a Village* (Clinton, 1996). It is an integral part of the person-in-environment framework used by social workers.

In the earlier section on family, it was noted that the family has a place in the community and the identity and image of the family in this wider context strongly affects every member in it. However, especially as a child grows and moves out into the world of community independently, a direct relationship also develops between that child and the members, groups, and organizations within the community.

The role of religious affiliation is particularly important in identity development. A strong religious affiliation will provide a clear set of values and a distinct worldview, grounded in religious faith, and encourage the development of particular personality traits and characteristics. Religious leaders can be strong role models throughout life as well. However, the perception of the wider community of the religious affiliation, and the particular experiences of each individual, can affect and mitigate some of these positive effects.

The College Years

Though significant work in identity development occurs in childhood, the college years are formative years as well. From high school, you selected (more or less independently, depending on your personal circumstances) the college you attended. Visits to college campuses immediately reveal the "flavor" of a school—and that of each school is different and unique. During the college years, the influence of teachers continues, as does the influence of peers.

At college, the years of earlier experience provide a foundation on which a firmer and surer sense of identity is developed. For many students, college is the first exposure to differences and diversity of all kinds, the first awareness that there may have been errors, or distortions, in some of the things that one was taught. In college, students are supposed to learn to "think on their own," to draw their own conclusions about things and people based on their own experiences. The degree of congruence between what a college student has experienced and been taught in childhood and adolescence and what is actually experienced in college may vary.

The Workplace

Another strong potential influence on identity development and self-image comes from experiences with employment. Bosses and supervisors, colleagues and coworkers interact, often for long hours, sharing not only coffee break conversations but also tasks. We measure our skill and ability level, evaluate our accomplishments, establish collegial relationships in the process of work.
"The workplace is often an arena where friendships are made," and

> many workers experience supportive relationships at the workplace, others find their relationships with workmates, supervisors, or supervisees difficult because of job stress or because of personal and interpersonal factors such as anxieties, ambivalences, problem attitudes toward authority and control, high performance expectations held by oneself or others, and the sexual harassment of working women by male supervisors or coworkers (the reverse is thought to be rare). Sexual harassment is a severe psychological stressor still experienced by many working women despite the laws in place. (Germain, 1991)

While public policy attempts to address these issues, individuals at times experience injustice and unfairness in treatment, hours, pay, or workspace. They must decide whether, and how, to advocate for themselves—to ask for a raise, to challenge the time allotted for an assignment, to report harassment, to ask for a better-lit workstation. Employees must decide how to deal with issues independently—away from the didactic environment of school and home, which allowed for and accepted errors.

From the manner in which we handle challenges at work and relate to others in that environment, we draw impressions of ourselves that contribute to our self-evaluation. We are also judged by others: some whose opinions we value.

Chapter Exercise

The objective of this chapter is to help you recognize the impact of others on the development of your identity.

1. List all of the members of your family, including extended and "honorary" family members you believe had an impact on your values and beliefs, worldview, interests, abilities, and personal characteristics. Beside their name, note as specifically as you can in what ways they influenced you. Note whether you perceive the influence on your identity as strong or weak, positive or negative.

2. List any teachers (elementary through college) whose effect on you was important. They might have inspired you to high achievement, diagnosed a learning disability, taught you self-control and punctuality, or perhaps inspired you to discover a new field of endeavor. You may not be able to recall all of the teachers who influenced your identity development: just do the best you can!

3. To create a division (which may be quite arbitrary), develop four sections labeled elementary school, middle school, high school, and college. In each section, list the peers who had a strong impact on you. Note the kind of impact and whether it is felt strongly or weakly today.

4. List any others who, you feel, had a strong influence on you. You can include employers; ministers, priests, or rabbis; group leaders; coworkers; etc. Note the impact each had on you and whether it is strongly or weakly felt today.

Chapter EIGHT

Exploring "Other"

Discomfort, curiosity, fascination, integration, stereotyping, bias, prejudice, alinenation, fear, shame, and hostility encompass only a few of the complex and myriad emotions we experience when we confront "other." Often, we experience several, perhaps conflicting, emotions simultaneously. At times, we are aware of our feelings, while at other times, they seem hardly accessible to us.

Gestalt psychology postulates that human beings are interested and involved with the world around themselves. Each person "organizes" the world into a coherent, consistent, and balanced whole (Hraba, 1994).

As we develop this organized view, we tend to categorize things and people, a process termed *perceptual grouping* in Gestalt psychology. As we do this, we tend to accentuate similarities among members of the categories we develop, and dissimilarity between the various groupings. This is termed the *assimilation/contrast principle,* a very useful concept for understanding our personal categorization of "we" and "they."

Behavioral theory suggests that such concepts as "we" and "they" are not innate. They are learned through conditioning, either by association or reinforcement. Thus, our experiences with "other" and the things that we have been told as we were growing up have a strong impact on our perceptions.

"We": A Sometimes Shifting Concept

Chapters 6 and 7 have provided a framework for understanding and acknowledging personal identity, and for exploring the various life encounters that have influenced the perception of this identity. You have examined both the positive and negative qualities by which you define yourself.

We also have begun to explore the concept of "we-ness" and suggested that this is often contextual. Each of us belongs to many different populations, and we identify with different groups under different circumstances. "We-ness" gives us a sense of community, of group membership, and therefore, of an identity that we share with others. We tend to congregate in groups and enjoy the feeling of association with others.

However, we often seem to prefer others who are similar to ourselves in some way. We enjoy the sense of sharing an identity and derive mutual support from others we view as similar to ourselves.

Our sense of "we-ness" expands and contracts depending on circumstances. For example, at an ecumenical service, "we" are Christians. In a Christian group, "we" are Protestants. In a Protestant group, "we" and Methodists.

If we are traveling out of the country, "we" are Americans. If we are with a group of people from all over the Americas, "we" are North Americans or citizens of the United States. Narrowing further makes "us" identify ourselves as Texans. Traveling in Texas, "we" are people from Houston.

At school, "we" are students. However, "we" are graduate students, or "we" are Seniors. "We" can also be students majoring in social work or students seeking an advanced social work degree.

We can reverse the order and say "we" are child welfare workers at Child Protective Services, a county agency in Cook County, Illinois. Expanding the category, "we" become social workers in a public agency in Cook County, Illinois. Depending on our circumstances, "we" can also be social workers from Illinois, social workers employed in public agencies, or child welfare workers.

This exercise can be done with any group or affiliation with which we identify, including race, gender, religion, ethnicity, age, class, sexual orientation, appearance, worldview, handicapping condition, and other, limitless possibilities.

"We-ness," however, by its very nature tends to be exclusionary. If there is a "we," there is also a "not-we"—a "they" or an "other."

"Other": A Question of Definition

Each of us functions daily within this shifting concept of "we," adjusting ourselves automatically as needed to the changes in our circumstances. This seems a simple process, but the simplicity may be deceiving!

If "we," by my own choice and definition, is "all Italian Americans," how am I going to define that? Do I mean "all first-generation immigrants from Italy"? Do I mean "all people of Italian ancestry"? Do I mean "everyone whose father and mother are Italian"? Or "everyone who identifies themselves as Italian American"? Perhaps I might mean "everyone that the Order of the Sons of Italy recognizes as Italian American"? Even "everyone that the dominant society determines is Italian-American" is a clear possibility—one, in fact, frequently used in the public forum.

The difficulties here are clearly manifested. Does each individual decide for him or herself group affiliation or membership in a particular population? Do members of the population decide who may, and who may not, be a part of that population? Does the leadership, hierarchy, or organizational structure within the population decide? Does the dominant society decide?

Each of these choices has many implications for the individual involved. Only the first allows for free choice. In each of the other possibilities, someone *else* defines the individual's identity in this vital area of group affiliation and membership.

When someone else defines an individual, the definer assumes a position of power and control, thereby creating an imbalance in the relationship between them. This imbalance, or disequilibrium, enables oppression to occur, and/or vulnerability to become oppression.

Thus, the separation between "we" and "other" or "they" contains the possibility of oppression. As social workers dedicated to work with at-risk, disempowered, and oppressed populations, it is important for us to understand not only how this separation and imbalance occurs, but also where we can place ourselves.

In common with all of humanity we, too, are sometimes defined and categorized by others. In attempting to understand personal identity in the previous chapters, we explored how our self-concept and self-definition have been formed, influenced, and defined by others in our environment in very powerful and sometimes painful ways, as well as in some very positive and helpful ones.

We are defined, and we also define. We all partake in the process of deciding who is a part of our group, or population, and who is not.

"Other": A Mysterious Entity

"Other" may be many things. However, it is *always* one thing: "not-us." Other is *by definition* something different from us.

It is difficult to imagine human beings prior to recorded history. We know them from the implements they left behind and the traces of civilization, community life, and creative expression. In these, all over the world, we find the traces of war.

What could these early human beings have been fighting about? There was, in general, ample land and resources for hunting, fishing, spaces for building communities, materials for tool making, and freedom for developing beliefs. The water was clean, the air pure, and the necessary resources available to all.

Several philosophers and anthropologists suggest that wars may have been fought simply because of this identification of certain groups as "other." "Other" is alien, unknown, unpredictable, and mysterious. "Other" can be fearsome or strange and have unknown and malignant powers. "Other" can arouse hostility by difference alone. Because "other" is unknown and unpredictable, humans have the tendency to avoid associating with those so designated. Of course, this lack of contact, experience, and knowledge of "other" encourages speculation and mistaken beliefs about differences.

"Other": Difference, Beliefs, and Feelings

Questions about the origin of the world, about the sun and moon and planets have interested humans since the beginning of time. Preclassical Greek civilization, the ancient Incas, the Mayan culture, the Egyptians, and the Chinese are but a few of the many early cultures that developed a complex system of belief to explain the universe. Time, study, and technology that have increased our knowledge and experience with the universe have proved some of these ideas to be in error, and modern civilization has amended, expanded, or abandoned these ancient systems.

When we do not know something, we tend to develop a system of belief about that thing, often drawn erroneously from speculation based on mistaken perception. The permutations drawn from this original error grow. The more they grow, the more certain we become of their correctness, and the more attached we become to the beliefs themselves.

"Progress," as we define it today, is built on knowledge and experience, on reason, and on the willingness to keep open the possibility of change and errors in previous thought.

We, too, have accepted a set of beliefs about "other"—beliefs based not on knowledge, contact, or experience, but on what we have been told and on what we have absorbed from the society around us.

Long, long before we made a commitment to social work and accepted the profession's commitment to work with disempowered and oppressed populations, we developed a set of beliefs about the things and the people that we did not know through reason, direct experience, and learning. Like our less-scientifically developed forbears, we are attached to our beliefs and find it hard to change them. The possibility for change suggested is, after all, profound: it is a change not only in what we believe but in how we see *ourselves* in relation to those beliefs.

Old shoes are comfortable; so are old beliefs. New ones often are quite painful at first; so are new beliefs.

One of the difficulties we might experience as we consider "other" and our perceptions of other is that along with internalized beliefs about "other" and the relationship between "other" and "us" are feelings, often very strong and powerful feelings, which are tenaciously attached to these beliefs. We have many feelings about "other." These may depend on the circumstances, our experiences, and what we have heard of or been taught.

A few of the possible feelings we might have are:

Curiosity

Fascination

Integration

Discomfort

Alienation

Fear

Shame

Hostility

Acceptance

Wariness

Anger

Hatred

Love

All people have some of these feelings about "other" at certain times. If you find, as you work through the chapter exercise, that you have many of the more negative feelings on this list, you may feel a desire to change or eliminate them immediately. Remember, it took all of your life for these feelings to reach this state. It will take a long time to change them. It is a worthwhile goal to desire to change them and a lifelong task to achieve some of these changes.

Learning about "Other"

We absorb our definitions of "other" from the world around us and from our experiences. This process begins while we are very young, and the early influence of parents and family, teachers, and peers is often significant.

In addition to what we are told, overhear, and observe, we also have direct experiences with "others" at times. Because we are usually quite young when these beliefs are formed and our ability to reason is not fully developed, we may draw erroneous conclusions from these experiences.

Along with our own errors, we also absorb the biases, prejudices, and stereotypes of those around us, especially those in a position of power, and those we respect. We develop a set of expectations about "other" and validate the experiences that support them while discounting those that do not.

As we grow older, we often forget some of these early experiences—the words we heard and the things we were told. We lose our awareness of why we think as we do about certain populations or groups of people. It sometimes seems, indeed, as though our deepest beliefs and feelings about "other" are so much a part of the fabric of who *we* are that it is impossible to disconnect them.

Chapter Exercise

We have explored some of the possible origins of the understanding of "other" and the beliefs and feelings that develop from these origins. This exercise will ask you to recall as much as you can about what you "learned" about "other."

In order to organize this section in a consistent manner, we shall follow the population categories defined earlier when you were exploring your self-identity. Make a copy of your group affiliation/population identity as you developed it in Chapter 6. Place it next to each category as you work on this exercise.

In each category, write what you perceive to be "other." You may have as many "others" in each category as you wish. Next to each group, write what you recall hearing, seeing, and experiencing about this particular "other" as you were growing up. If possible, note who, where, and how you felt.

Gender:

Age:

Race:

Ethnicity:

Class:

Religious affiliation:

Sexual orientation:

Refugee, immigrant, undocumented alien status:

Education:

Handicapping conditions:

Region or section of country:

Unit II Summary

This unit explored aspects of personal identity and asked you to undertake a personal journey of self-awareness in order to gain an awareness of your own identity, in terms of both personal and group affiliations, and of the events, experiences, and people that helped shape it. We then took the first steps of the journey outward from self, a journey that explored ideas about what and who we consider as "other" and the reasons for these delineations.

In Chapter 5, we briefly reviewed some of the major theories of identity development to establish a framework within which to examine and explore ourselves and our personal identity development.

As we began self-exploration in Chapter 6, we maintained the "inner and outer framework" concept that we used in the first unit. We explored, first, the inner framework: the personal, individual, and often very private aspects of personal identity. Then, we moved toward the outer framework: that part of our identity that we hold in common with others. This consists of our various group affiliations.

Having established some sense of awareness about identity, we proceeded to explore in Chapter 7 some of the people, events, and experiences that were instrumental in the development of our self-concept and personal identity, proceeding chronologically from early childhood to adulthood. We explored both the negative and the positive effects of these outside influences on our concept of self.

Armed with an awareness and understanding of self and identity, Chapter 8 asked that we consider how and why we define certain groups or individuals as "other" by exploring the manner in which human beings see "we" and "they," a uniquely human manner of thinking about people and things. We used the information and affiliations from Chapter 6, about ourselves, to arrive at a specific idea of "they."

The work of this unit has been completely focused on you, on increasing your self-awareness of who, what, and why you are as you are, and on understanding who and what you consider different from yourself and why. This has been a difficult but rewarding task.

In the next unit, we will return to the mission and goals of the profession and your own as an aspiring professional. We will explore these in the context of the awareness gained in this unit.

Unit II Assignment

Personal Identity

The preceding chapters have helped you explore the fascinating and complex subject of identity development and self-identity. You have worked on defining yourself in terms of your unique experiences, as well as your group identifications.

In a paper approximately three pages in length, present what you feel are the most important elements of your self-identity, both as an individual and in terms of group affiliation. You may use some of the categories or groupings included in previous chapter exercises or organize your paper according to your own priorities and values.

It is recognized that there may be some very personal information included in your self-identity: include only what, or as much as, you are comfortable disclosing. For personal growth and awareness, however, do think about *why* you have chosen to include or omit some part of your personal identity. You will learn much about yourself from your reasons!

You may want to begin with broad categories, such as "I am a Hispanic woman of Central American origin," or "My family emigrated to this country four generations ago, but I have not maintained any ethnic ties. I consider myself an American," and move on to the personal and unique characteristics, such as "I enjoy singing and sing in a chorus," or "I have always been considered the oldest, most responsible child in my family," or "I believe that the limited circumstances in which I grew up help me to understand other poor people."

You may write your paper on the following pages, or use them to organize and order your thoughts.

Unit III

Developing a Model
for Growth and Change

Unit III takes each of us on an exciting journey: a journey toward "other." Unlike Units I and II, which asked that you think, reflect, define, and explore, this unit will ask that you also *do*.

There is not a person in this world, not a single one, who does not hold a sense of "we" and "other," and who does not, in some manner and at some level, associate some negativity with these feelings toward "other." We call them biases, prejudices, or stereotypes.

Sometimes we are well aware of them and accept them. Sometimes we work hard to fight against them and seek to purge our minds and hearts of them. Sometimes we are not aware: these feelings are buried deep within us, hidden under a canopy of "acceptable" excuses or rationales.

For us as professional social workers, the definition of "we" and "they" impacts strongly upon the work that we do. It affects how we assess our clients and their problems, the interventions we choose, and the goals we set. Do we want our clients to become "more like us" as the charity organization society ladies did, or do we want them to become "more what they want to be"?

To help them toward "what they want to be," we must be willing to hear and see the world through their experiences—not an easy task if their experiences are very different from ours.

Chapter 9 brings us back to the work of Unit I; however, we will examine our personal and professional values and goals in a fuller and deeper context: that of our own identity and of our concept of "other." In Chapter 10, we will practice a model for change and growth by reaching out toward a self-selected "other" population on several different levels. We will process our experience through the writing and discussion work of Chapter 11 and consider the possibilities for use of the model in different contexts in Chapter 12. Hopefully, we will each reach the end of Unit III understanding the possibility for change in our concept of "other" and with a recognition of the value of that change.

In this unit, you will be asked to open your mind, your eyes and ears, and your heart and take a beginning step toward "other." You will find this a rewarding and exhilarating experience.

Chapter NINE

Viewing "Other" through the Lens of Professional and Personal Values and Commitments

The work of the preceding chapters has required intense self-exploration and, at times, a painful honesty. We have explored personal identity on an individual level and in terms of group membership and affiliation. We have attempted to understand not only *who* we are, but *how* we came to be who we are in terms of our values, worldview, beliefs, personal characteristics, and group identifications and affiliations. We have explored the ideas and the feelings that accompany a sense of "we-ness", and also what "other" means to us personally. We have tried to examine the origin of some of our ideas and beliefs about "other."

Negative stereotypes, biases, and prejudices are often a part of our beliefs and feelings about "other." Sometimes, we are aware of these negative characteristics that we ascribe to others. At other times, they are deeply buried in our subconscious, in our language, in our gestures, and in our behavior.

In addition, discrimination, prejudice, and oppressive conditions in our society are often embedded in laws, policies, traditions, and customs, and reflected in our institutions, making it more difficult for an individual to be fully aware of the exclusion of certain members of society from the general welfare of all. Institutionalized oppression often insidiously validates the claims of the oppressor to conditions of privilege and power.

In this chapter, we will return to the basic values and commitments of the profession and to our own values. We will explore these values and commitments in terms of the way we have learned to view "other." We will consider whether our commitments—to the profession and to our vision of ourselves—ask that we reevaluate and reassess some of our beliefs and experiences.

Effecting change is a complex and difficult task. In order to understand our ability to achieve the changes we desire to make, we will consider the strengths we bring with us to this endeavor.

Professional Values and Commitments

As we have seen, the values of the social work profession strongly support social justice and the dignity and worth of individuals. Thus, the profession undertakes a special commitment to vulnerable, at-risk, disempowered, and oppressed populations. There is a commitment to social action and to efforts to empower individuals and groups who are suffering from discrimination, prejudice, and oppression. Social workers are also committed to the support of policies and laws that respect and consider differences among and between peoples.

On a personal level, each social worker carries a commitment to learning about cultures, ethnicities, beliefs, customs, and behaviors of the client population the worker is serving. As noted earlier, this is the intellectual part of the professional commitment.

However, there is also a professional obligation to awareness of the worker's individual values, cultural, religious, and other beliefs, and of the impact of these beliefs on professional comportment. As you moved through the work of the preceding chapters, you have been endeavoring to meet this obligation through self-exploration and awareness of your feelings and beliefs about others. At present, hopefully, you have attained an in-depth view of yourself and the way you relate to difference.

Personal Values and Commitments

As a part of the process of self-exploration, you have noted the congruence between the professional value base of social work and your personal values and beliefs. As you explored your identity, you also examined, defined, and attempted to hierarchize your personal value system.

Your personal hierarchy probably included values such as justice, fairness, freedom, good life quality, dignity and respect, happiness, and equality. You may also have included knowledge and education, religion, faith or spirituality, pleasant employment, leisure, care for others, friendship, love, and health.

If you have discussed values with another person, you may have noticed that many of the words you choose to describe values are the same. You may have reflected wonderingly on the fact that, although you and your friend both value "equality," you define it differently.

Employment and college admission are two areas where the definition of "equality" has been hotly debated in recent times. "Equality" can mean that everyone has a right to apply and that those best qualified, able to perform, able to pay, etc. get the jobs and the college places. "Equality" also can mean leveling the playing field before such competition begins, giving those who have suffered disadvantages in education, skills training, financial resources, opportunities, or discrimination certain advantages to make the competition more equal. This has been called "affirmative action."

Some have argued that affirmative action is a practical and workable system to mitigate past or present disadvantages that affect certain members of society in a negative manner, thus enabling them to enjoy some of the benefits commonly associated with life in these United States. Others argue that affirmative action may result in "reverse discrimination"—that some who would otherwise have obtained the admission or position they were seeking were denied in favor of a less-qualified applicant who receives special consideration through affirmative action.

When you consider values, it is important to try to define what you mean by the general term you use. It is helpful to discuss these definitions with friends, fellow-students, and colleagues. Not only will this get them thinking about this important subject, it will also help you clarify what you mean by the value term you use by the necessity of explaining it to them!

Although there are individual differences among our personal values, there are many similarities as well. Philosophers generally agree that human beings seek something that is generally defined as "happiness." This happiness is not a thing of peak moments, such as a great evening with friends, a wonderful love relationship, or an achievement at work. Rather, the kind of happiness that all people seek is a quality that pervades the entire span of a lifetime—a happiness that recognizes that there may be bad and painful times in life but that one's life, as a whole, is good and is worth living.

Recognizing Conflict: Our Values and "Other"

Bringing "other" into the discussion of professional and personal values presents a vital dimension to our work of self-awareness.

If I value these things, you must ask yourself, do I value them only for myself, or do I believe that *everyone* is entitled to them? Do I allow myself to define my values only, or do I recognize that others, too, have the right to define their values for themselves? Are there values, within my own values, that support freedom, equality, justice, dignity, and worth not just for me, but for everyone? What about education, good life quality, and pleasant employment? If I have the right to try to attain happiness, however I define it, does every other human being have this right as well?

Added to this personal level are the core values of the profession, especially those of social justice and the dignity and worth of each individual. A commitment to the profession implies not only acceptance and support, but also a strong commitment to and advocacy for those values.

Often, however, there is a division in our perception of values, goals, ideals, and behavior. When we try to place ourselves along the continuum developed on page 79, we may find that our professional and personal goals and commitments fall generally within the category of the "me" who functions smoothly in everyday life but that there are areas where there is a distinct pull between the personal ideals and values we espouse and how we behave and react in certain situations.

Often, the places where there is the greatest conflict, the greatest pull, center around the distinction between our values, in an ideal sense, and our daily functioning, especially in regard to our attitudes, beliefs, and feelings about "other." We may, for example, espouse racial integration but live in a segregated neighborhood. We may advocate for acceptance of ethnic diversity but have immediately expressed the belief, after the bombing of the Murrah State Office Building in Oklahoma City, that it was undoubtedly an Arab terrorist attack. We may believe that all people are to be treated with respect but talk disparagingly about someone we think is "crazy," or "not right in the head." We may believe that "family" includes many forms of living arrangements and personal bonds but not want our children playing at "those lesbians' house."

We may believe that men and women should have equal rights but hire the woman because "everyone knows women are better nurses—after all, women are the nurturers!" We may hire the 20 year old over the 50 year old because "everyone knows old people are set in their ways." If we are white, we may hire the white person because "everyone knows blacks can't spell, and they're never on time" or "because everyone says those Hispanics look so cheap in their high heels."

The theme running through these examples is, of course, the "everyone knows." This is the source of legitimization for the action, belief, or position being taken. "Everyone" lends a statement power and validity. Who is "everyone"? Is it truly "everyone" or really "all of us" or "we"?

We may also, if Hispanic hire the Hispanic, because "they're just like me"; if black, hire the white because "I don't want to be accused of hiring someone just because of color"; or if Japanese, hire the Japanese because "they know the proper way to behave." These reasons, too, come from within the concept of "we" and how "we" expects us to think, believe, and behave.

"Other" is often the butt of our jokes. There are Polish jokes, Irish jokes, black jokes, Jewish jokes, Catholic jokes, Arab jokes, and women jokes. There are also old people jokes and mentally ill jokes and disabled person jokes and homosexual jokes. There are few, very few, dominant population jokes, even among the minority and oppressed populations themselves.

All of us have been exposed to these kinds of jokes and attitudes all of our lives. We may even have actively participated and contributed a joke of our own. As you read this, that very moment and that very recollection may be burning in your memory. The remarks, the jokes, the attitudes expressed generally all have one feature in common: *they are always told among "us" and are always about "them."*

Our responses to the jokes, remarks, behaviors, and actions of others often vary by circumstance and context. We can join in or add a comment of our own. We can maintain silence. We can walk away. We can object.

Often, we would like to object. Our values and goals, our ideals and personal beliefs, even our personal life experiences seem to demand that we object. Objection, however, is not a simple decision to make, because in this value-laden and potentially explosive area, objection often carries far-reaching effects. Objectors take risks.

There is the possibility of engaging in a serious argument and finding oneself isolated from the "we" that was a pleasant dinner conversation among friends. There is the possibility of offending and even challenging the authority of parents and other family members to whom you owe respect. There is the possibility of being ostracized at work for siding with "them" or of losing a great new opportunity for having objected to the boss's statements.

If the way you choose to react to these painful and difficult situations is not in harmony with your personal values and with your professional commitment, you will feel a sense of tension and frustration within. When this happens, it is time to draw back, reassess, and reevaluate your beliefs, commitments, and perhaps even your relationships.

It may be that you will find that there are circumstances where you must speak out, where you must advocate. There may be others where you feel withdrawal or silence is appropriate: the risk is too great, the circumstance too trivial, the remark possible to have been misinterpreted. These are very difficult and very personal decisions and require a great deal of thought.

It will help greatly if you think about your responses, and the possible circumstances, before they occur. In this way, you will be more comfortable and more able to act in accordance with your values and beliefs.

Assessing the Commitment for Change

More difficult than determining what to do in situations where you are exposed to oppression of others but are not yourself actively participating in the oppression are the situations where you find deep within yourself a stereotype, prejudice, fear, or belief about "other" that causes *you* to discriminate, avoid, condone inequity and oppression of others, disregard, or invalidate. It may be that, at times, these thoughts are buried so deeply within you that you are not aware of them. As you continue in your studies for the social work profession, you may find yourself uncovering more and more of them.

Shame and humiliation often immediately follow the thought. "How can I think this?" you cry to yourself, "I *know* better. I'm a social worker. I want to *help* people."

Yes, you do, and you can and will.

You are taking the steps you need to take to enable yourself to do that in the process of completing this workbook.

There are strengths, traits of character, values, and ideals within you that will enable you to make the changes in yourself that you believe you need to make. You have them already: you have a concern and respect for others, a commitment to the dignity of human beings, a sense of social justice, a willingness to advocate for others. These are all essential, as are the following traits:

Openness. The first, most basic element in assessing your ability to change and your strengths is to examine your ability to be open to others, to really *listen,* and to hear what others are saying.

Acceptance. It is important to be able to accept the things that "others" tell you as valid. You must recognize that other persons' views of the world may be just as valid for *them* as yours is *for you.*

Willingness. This is not a process that can be "forced" on anyone. There must be a willingness to listen, learn, and change attitudes and perceptions.

Trust. Exploring and learning about "other" requires that you trust, because you cannot allow yourself the experience that you need if you are unable to trust.

Knowledge. The more you know about another group, the more you are able to understand the group's experience and worldview. You can learn from books, the media, or directly from members of the group.

Interest. If you have a sincere and genuine interest in a group or population, this will manifest itself in your attitude and behavior, and encourage openness, trust, and sharing from others.

Courage. Working to change deeply held reactions and belief patterns is not an easy task. It's much simpler to just push them away or pretend to have the "politically correct" attitudes. It takes a great deal of personal courage to fully engage the task of change.

The possibility is within you. Enabling the possibility to come to be is essential to work with vulnerable and oppressed populations.

Chapter Exercise

1. List the personal strengths that you have that you believe will enable you to grow and to change, if necessary, some of the beliefs that you hold about "other."

2. What do you believe will be the strongest barriers to achieving change? These may be internal or external.

3. Who will be your allies as you try to redefine "other"? Where can you go for help and support?

Chapter TEN

A Model for Change

The recognition that a change in perception of "other" may be necessary and essential to becoming a competent and culturally sensitive social worker is very important. Openness toward all "others" will enable the optimal development of the helping relationship and will minimize some of the possible imbalances inherent in that relationship.

As noted earlier, the worker's perception of the client is particularly influential and important when the client or the worker are members of a perceived minority or of a vulnerable and oppressed population. Here, the imbalances inherent in the worker–client relationship can be magnified and distorted by both the client and the worker's perception of "other."

The worker may need to assist the client to address his or her perception of the "other" represented by the worker. However, the worker must also address his or her own perception of the "other" that is represented by the client. It is important that the worker begin this task, if possible, prior to initiating work with a client, so she may enter into the relationship with the maximum possible understanding and openness.

In this chapter, we will "practice" a model that may assist you in developing a different perception of "other" by engaging in a process of learning and relating to one of the populations that you have defined as "other." Though the process will include cognitive elements, the objective is primarily affective change.

> Note: It is important for you to recognize that the objective here is not a total change in beliefs and attitudes. This would not be possible for the majority of people, and it is not necessary to competent, professional practice.
>
> However, it *is* both necessary and possible, through self-awareness and experience, to control and to minimize attitudes and beliefs that may be harmful and prejudicial toward clients through increased understanding of their life experiences with disempowerment, bias, prejudice, and oppression.

Selecting a Population

You can select any population that you perceive to be vulnerable or oppressed for this project. The reasons for your choice are personal but should include one or more of the following:

- a population with whom you are working currently
- a population with whom you plan to work
- a population about whom you are aware that you hold stereotypes
- a population about whom you are aware that you hold negative biases, prejudices, or that you discriminate against
- a population about whom you are aware that influential people around you—parents, teachers, friends, employer, etc.—hold negative biases, prejudices, stereotypes, etc.
- a population that inspires fear, revulsion, hatred, shame, or other negative feeling within you

For this project do *not* choose:

- a population to which you believe you belong
- a population to which someone close to you belongs
- a population that interests you, fascinates you, or about whom you are curious

These restrictions will help you make this more than just an intellectual exercise or an experience in learning more about something or someone you already hold in positive regard. The object is to address some *negative* feelings and perceptions, and work to change them.

Intellectual Learning

Although the objective is not cognitive but affective change, learning the history of the population, its traditions, customs, and beliefs will help you recognize and acknowledge the validity of the population's experience and understand the potential effects of this on current members.

Learning from Literature and Film

The literature of a people reflects its inward experiences, feelings, worldview, and self-perception. Reading literature by members of a population about their experiences will assist you both to understand them on an emotional level and recognize the common humanity that binds you as an individual to that population.

Films, especially those written, produced, and directed by members of your selected population, can also assist you to envision clearly some aspect of the population's experience. There are many excellent films available. Some may take a little searching out, but that very process is a learning experience in itself!

Learning from Immersion

One of the ways to address some of the negative feelings and perceptions individuals have about "other" is to make "other" become more familiar. Sharing events, experiences, festivals, and religious services; trying special food or drink; exploring and understanding styles of clothing; and learning expressions both verbal and nonverbal are all valuable in increasing your experience of "other."

Learning from Individuals

Reaching out to an individual member of a population about whom you are experiencing internal conflict and possible negativity may be one of the most difficult steps in this project. Reaching out requires a strong faith in the other person's willingness to understand and share openly with you and in your own ability to handle possible rejection or negativity from the person.

Some suggestions for individuals who might be open to engage with you in this kind of project follow:

Fellow students

Coworkers

Casual acquaintances with whom you have experienced a good rapport

Leaders of community, ethnic, religious, or other organizations for which membership in the population is an essential criteria of membership in the group

Participants in multicultural groups, "diversity" groups, or other groups whose purpose is to discuss differences and relationships among groups

Because the objective here is *dialogue,* it is not sufficient that you be open to listening and supportive of what is being said; you, too, must be willing to share your experiences and perceptions of differences. This is a *mutual* process: it is *not* an interview.

Through these experiences and any others you believe might be helpful to you, you will reach a place where the distinct lines between "we" and "they," so clearly drawn in the exercises of earlier sections, begin to blur.

Chapter Exercise

This exercise will take some time. Be sure that you allow yourself to experience each of the parts as fully as possible.

1. Select a population.
2. Seek and read a history of the experiences of this population, at least over the past several centuries, including immigration experience to the United States, if applicable to the population *as a whole* (may not be useful for mental illness or disability, physical disability, etc. Native American history, though not one of immigration, can be helpful if you are electing to work with this population). This need not be a heavy tome, just reading that will acquaint you with the population's experience from a historical perspective. If a course you are taking includes an ethnicity textbook, focusing on the section that addresses your chosen population's experience will be very helpful.
3. Read at least one or two books *by* a member of the population or group you have selected. Look for well-known authors, who express their experience from an affective level as well as a cognitive level. Good literature will help you to gain insight and appreciation for the population you are working with. If possible, view a film that is written, produced, directed, and acted by members of the population.
4. Attend at least two events—religious, cultural, educational, experiential, or other—that are "of" the population you have selected. Examples include street fairs, religious services, group meetings, community association activities, etc. Go alone if you feel comfortable doing this, because it will provide a meaningful experience for you in *being* "other" in relation to that group and also allow for greater possibilities of interaction. However, if you are very uncomfortable attending alone, take a friend or colleague along with you. The object is to increase your level of comfort and interaction. Placing yourself in situations where you are *overly* uncomfortable will only increase the discomfort!
5. Engage several members of the population or group you have selected in a meaningful conversation about their experiences as a member of the group. If possible, introduce variety by choosing people of different ages, experiences, and conditions. In other words, select people who hold the quality that you have selected in common but have many other characteristics that are different.

Population I have selected:

Reasons for my choice:

Chapter ELEVEN

Reassessing "Other"

In the exercise of Chapter 10, you experienced relating to the population you selected on several levels and under various circumstances. Hopefully, your learning and experience has given you some new tools for understanding and relating to them.

Some of your new perceptions may support some of your old ones, and you may find congruity between them. However, you also will find that many of the experiences you have had have changed the way you view the chosen population.

In most instances, the books, activities, and people you have chosen to experience will have had a positive impact on your understanding of the population you selected. However, this may not have been the case in all instances: you may have had experiences of rejection, isolation, hostility, invisibility, or other uncomfortable feelings. You may have felt *yourself* disliked, stereotyped, and discriminated against.

It is possible to use these negative experiences to reinforce your previously held beliefs and attitudes about this population, or you can try to take the experiences apart, avoid generalizing, and look at each negative experience in the context in which it occurred. The circumstances will tell you a great deal about what you encountered.

Fear and mistrust, and thus avoidance, rejection, hostility, and anger are not yours alone. Minority, oppressed, poor, disempowered, and vulnerable populations of all kinds have the same kinds of concerns about "other" that you do. Oppression and vulnerability to "others" does not, *in itself,* erase the possibility of negative feelings toward differences of any kind. It may, in fact, even increase it! It is important for you to recognize this as directed toward the "other" that you represent, not at you *personally.*

If the population you have selected views *you* as an oppressor for any reason, your task may have been more difficult but certainly very worthwhile, because in reaching out to understand and being open to being understood, you have given as well as received the experience of trust, risk, and sharing.

It is probable, however, that most of your experiences with the exercise have been positive. You have gained an understanding of the selected population from close at hand: you have felt, seen, and touched life as it is being experienced by this group. You have, in a sense, entered into their experience. Hopefully, you will have found both something unique and of value, and something that attests to the commonalities between you.

Change has already begun and is still occurring. The change will not be sudden, nor will it be complete. This is not the kind of work where it is possible to say, "O.K., that's all done!" It took you many years, possibly your lifetime, to develop the beliefs and attitudes you had about this "other." It will take a long time to change them in a deep and truly permanent manner.

Writing Your Experience

You may have found yourself taking notes, jotting down ideas or experiences as you progressed through the work of Chapter 10. You may have preferred not to write but to just experience to the fullest.

Retrospectively writing some of your thoughts and feelings as you proceeded through the experiences of Chapter 10 will help you relive them and reassess them. You will be able to linger within a conversation, ponder a chance remark, or compare an event to something you have experienced previously. Writing will help you "fix" the things you learned more clearly in your mind, and it will enable you to go back and reread and reexperience them as often as you wish.

You will be writing about your experience in this chapter's exercise.

Sharing with Peers

There are wonderful opportunities for further growth and learning, and for deeper consideration and reflection, in sharing some of your experiences, reading, and conversations with fellow students. You will be able to share with those who have selected the same population the richness of the similarities and differences between your experiences. You will also be able to reflect together and to understand that what you each brought with you to the experiences, your unique values, worldview, personal characteristics, and life experiences have strongly influenced the way you approached the same population, the way you engaged with them, and the things that have had the greatest impact on you.

Discussion with fellow students who have selected a population different from yours will enable you to gain something from their learning and experience. It may stimulate you to repeat the exercise with another population. You will also be able to explore similarities and differences and include the commonalities fellow students have found in the broader understanding of the commonalities between all human beings.

Reexamining Your Feelings and Beliefs about Your Selected "Other"

To explore your new understanding and affirm any changes you have made, it is helpful to return to the section in Chapter 8 where you originally wrote your thoughts and beliefs about this particular population. You may wish to rewrite them separately from the other groups included in the Chapter 8 exercise.

Consider what you wrote carefully. Where did your attitudes and beliefs come from? How could the errors, fears, and mistrust have developed?

Compare these with the experiences of Chapter 10 with the selected population. While not discounting your earlier experiences and beliefs, attempt to integrate them with your new experiences. This is not a simple process. Far beyond the last session of this class and the last page of this workbook, the work of reconciliation will continue.

Sharing with Family Members, Friends, and Others

Deciding what, how much, and under what circumstances you will share your experience with those in your personal world, the "we's" with whom you shared the separation from "other," is a highly personal and individual task, one that should be undertaken with thought and care.

You have had a new experience, are filled with a new awareness, and have changed some of the beliefs and attitudes you shared with those who formed your "we." Perhaps, your "we" has expanded and grown.

Others have not had this experience. They may welcome your changes and be eager to share in them, learning from you and from your experience. They may be indifferent. They may not care or might withdraw from conversation about your experience. Hardest of all, they may reject, attempt to invalidate, or ridicule your experience. They may like their world as it is and not want change forced on them.

Only you can decide what will work best for each individual in your personal world. The risks, the rejection, the broadening of everyone's "we" concept is yours to determine. The only suggestion that can be offered here is that you consider carefully what and how the subject is addressed, understand the potential reactions you may receive, and prepare yourself to address those reactions to the best of your ability.

Chapter Exercise

1. As best you can, write some of what you have experienced and learned from the Chapter 10 exercise. You may wish to organize this by event, experience, author, etc., or by sphere, such as family life, culture, belief system, tradition, daily life experiences, interactions with members' "other," history, etc.

2. Re-read what you have written as often as you can. Add details you may have forgotten as they come to mind. Think about the experiences and try to put yourself in the place of the people you read about, spoke with, and visited. You will be able to do this by *using* what you have learned, your empathic skills, and your understanding of your common humanity.

3. Copy the section about your population that you had written in Chapter 8, and place it with your new perceptions. Compare both sections and search for changes, affirmations, and differences.

Chapter TWELVE

Self-Awareness as a Way of Life

Much of the work of education for the social work profession is cognitive: an intellectual grasping of theories, principles, techniques, and skills necessary for effective and competent practice. However, the work also involves the integration of the value base of the profession and its mission into the whole person of the developing professional and the recognition of the mutuality and congruence of personal and professional values.

This integration is vital to the development of professional social work identity. For some, the decision to become a social worker was a reasoned and reflective one, based on life experiences and interests. For others, it sprang from a desire to help others or to "make a difference in the world." Others view their entry into the profession truly as a calling that they felt deeply on an intuitive level. No matter what the reason for entering our profession, the work of integration of the personal and the professional value bases can affirm and validate that decision.

The profession's mission includes a deep and abiding commitment to the poor, vulnerable, oppressed, and disenfranchised. It is this mission that originally created the impetus for the development of the profession and that carries it forward into the challenges of today's complex and rapidly changing world.

We are each "special"—unique in very different and individual ways. However, there are groups of people, populations, that *as a whole* are special. Specialness causes feelings of difference and awareness of "self" and "other." Some kinds of specialness are viewed as positive by the individuals who are special, by those around them, and by the general population. Other kinds of specialness have negative connotations and create many difficulties and obstacles for those who have these qualities. Vulnerable, at-risk, and oppressed populations often suffer from this negative kind of specialness.

Because as social workers we are each, alone and together as a profession, committed to these populations, it is essential that we understand both ourselves and the populations in the sense of this specialness. This can be accomplished only through an increased level of self-awareness, an understanding of our own identity and of what it means to be someone different from ourselves.

We learn this on the individual level through theories about human development and behavior, and theories of growth and change. We learn this on a group or population level through theories of socialization, group behavior, culture and acculturation, and oppression.

The task of this workbook has been a different kind of learning: the development of self-awareness. This is an arduous but very rewarding project, and it is hoped that the work you have done in the previous chapters of this book have affirmed this for you.

Affirming Personal Identity

From a consideration of theories of identity development, we have moved through the process of identifying, clarifying, and defining our individual identities. We have noted that there are aspects of our identity that belong to us alone and aspects we share with others, the "we" with whom we consider ourselves affiliated by choice or by ascription.

We have also explored external influences on the development of our identities: the influences of parents, siblings, and other family members; teachers and group leaders; friends, neighbors, and peers; members of our communities; employers and colleagues. We have worked to become aware of the extent of both positive and negative effects that each has had on the development of our self-identity.

Defining "Other"

The exploration of "other" has shown us that "other" is defined differently by every person. "Other" is "they," "not-me," "different." With the difference often comes feelings and beliefs and attitudes.

Simply by virtue of being "other," those we consider in this way are unknown to us in a true sense. We, therefore, develop a perception of these "others" drawn from things we have been told, overheard, seen, or experienced.

Often, "other" is regarded with anxiety, and distrust is drawn simply from lack of experience, knowledge, and information. At other times, "other" may be the subject of more intense emotions and beliefs: hatred, hostility, disgust, and fear.

Changing Our Definitions

When "other" is a population to whom we are professionally committed, there is a special responsibility to that population to explore and, if necessary, change some of the perhaps mistaken perceptions about "other" and the negative feelings and emotions that accompany them.

This commitment carries with it the obligation both to learn about the population so regarded and to reconsider one's own perceptions in light of this learning. The process you have experienced, of reading, discussion, and experiential immersion, has given you the opportunity to learn and reconsider. Thus, you have been able to develop an understanding of the "other" you have selected for this project based more truly on the experiences and characteristics of the population.

Content and Process: Familiar Terms in a New Context

Content and process are terms familiar to social workers at every level of the profession. The simultaneous awareness of both content and process, and the ability to work within both, are some of the most important skills a worker brings to the client–worker encounter. There has been a content and a process to the experience of "other" as well.

The "content" has been the particular population you have selected and what you have learned and experienced about them. The content contains both the ideas you brought with you when you began your work and new or changed ideas that have developed.

The "process" is the way you went about the learning and changing. The process included the definition of "self" and "other," and the steps you took in exploring the population you selected: reading about their history, reading literature from members of the population or group, immersing yourself in the group's world or environment and experiencing *with* them, and talking with individuals in your selected population and sharing experiences and thoughts.

The "content" that you learned will assist you in working with the chosen group. You will be able to add many layers of "content" to those you have built, gaining a deeper understanding of the experiences and world of this vulnerable and oppressed group.

Using the "Process"

The "process," however, can be used over and over, with and on behalf of any group you consider to be "other" and wish to explore and experience in a more direct and authentic manner. The "process" can be used with any of the groups you defined as "other" as you were working through Chapter 8.

The "process" is there for you. You can apply it to both your professional and personal life. You can teach it to others and share it with friends and colleagues.

As you use the "process" over and over, you will find it easy to take a few shortcuts. Your self-identity will be affirmed, and the work of redefinition need not be undertaken each time. You will have an understanding of the persons and events that influenced your perceptions and may not need to redevelop this part of the process. It is important, however, that you try, in so far as it is possible to you, to follow all of the steps outlined in Chapter 11 in order to maximize your opportunity to learn, grow, and change.

Developing a "Wider Identity"

As you work through the process of changing your perception of "other," you will find that you develop a wider concept of your own identity.

"Wider identity," Pinderhughes notes, "refers to identity that transcends small collectivity boundaries and centers on identity as a world citizen. Erikson considers such identity characteristic of the highest level of functioning" (Pinderhughes, 1990, p. 45).

For social workers, widening the perception of self-identity enables a more inclusive relationship with those previously perceived as "other." This will foster the establishment of a positive working relationship with clients, as well as enhance the possibilities for personal growth and life experiences.

Self-Awareness Is a Lifelong Project

From birth, we begin the process of self-awareness, of the development and understanding of the concept of "me" and "not-me," and its implication for the world in which we live. For the infant, the world is all "me." There is at first no awareness of where "self" ends and other begins. Awareness progresses from physical to mental to emotional as growth proceeds.

As we extend our awareness outward, we also move from "me" and "not-me" to "we" and "not-we." This is a natural part of the way our minds work: we categorize things as similar and different, just as we categorize them as one or many, present or not present, etc.

Problems begin when we learn to associate negative beliefs, attributes, and attitudes with "not-we," "other," or "them." We create a separation that is not simply difference, but a negative, dividing, conflicting difference. It is this layer of separation, the negative, mistrustful layer, that we must work to change and guard ourselves against so we can fulfill both our image of ourselves, and our mission to our profession.

There is no exercise at the conclusion of this chapter. The exercise for this chapter is your commitment to self-awareness—for the rest of your life.

Unit III Summary

The work of this unit has asked that you embark on an exploration of a specific "other," and work toward a possible redefinition and reassessment of your values, attitudes, and beliefs about that "other."

The rationale for the work you have done was grounded in Chapter 9, which asked you to review the mission, goals, and values of the social work profession and of yourself as an aspiring social worker. These must be placed within the personal identity framework that you carry with you: your unique life experiences and worldview, your group affiliations and memberships, and your concept of "we" and "they."

During this exploration, we each in our own way noted that there were inconsistencies. Our values, goals, and ideals often become lost or partially obscured by the exigencies of our daily lives. We espouse social justice and equality, but some of our personal beliefs and attitudes toward others belie these values. Recognizing and addressing these inconsistencies is particularly important for social workers because of the intimate connection that exists between "we" and "they" in the context of the client-worker relationship, already prone toward imbalances that favor the worker in terms of knowledge, power, and authority.

A model for growth and change was developed and chronicled in Chapters 10 and 11. You were asked to select a population, and read, study, discuss, and experience that population in a very immediate and intimate way. The underlying rationale here was that knowledge and experience help us modify the stereotypes, biases, and prejudices born out of ignorance and fear.

It is hoped that the experience of this model and the exercises it involved were a rewarding and positive one for you and that you will be able to carry and apply the model to other life circumstances as you move through your professional careers, as well as your personal lives.

Unit III Assignment

Application of the Change Model

In a paper approximately five pages in length, describe your experiences and what you learned as you used the model for growth and change in relation to the population you selected. Include a description of the event that you attended; the book that you read; the film that you saw; and the people with whom you spoke. How did you react to the experiences? In what manner did they change or increase your understanding of the population you selected?

As a summation of this semester's affective work, describe what you learned in the process of working through this workbook.

Blank pages are provided to assist you in developing an outline for this paper.

References

Addams, J. (1910). *Twenty years at Hull House.* New York: Macmillan.

Addams, J. (1930). *The second twenty years at Hull House.* New York: Macmillan.

Allen, P. G. (1992). Angry women are building: Issues and struggles facing American Indian women today. In M. L. Anderson & P. H. Collins (Eds.), *Race, class, and gender.* Belmont, CA: Wadsworth Publishing Co.

Arredondo, P. M. (1984). Identity themes for immigrant young adults. *Adolescence, 14*(76), 977–93.

Betances, S. (1992). Race and the search for identity. In M. L. Anderson & P. H. Collins (Eds.), *Race, class, and gender.* Belmont, CA: Wadsworth Publishing Co.

Bisman, C. (1994). *Social work practice.* Pacific Grove, CA: Brooks/Cole Publishing Co.

Bok, S. (1989). *Lying: Moral choice in public and private life.* New York: Vintage Books.

Bulhan, H. A. (1985). *Franz Fanon and the psychology of oppression.* New York: Plenum Press.

Canda, E. R. (1991). East/west philosophical synthesis in transpersonal theory. *Journal of Sociology and Social Welfare, 18*(4), 137–52.

Clinton, H. R. (1996). *It takes a village.* New York: Touchstone Books.

Code of Ethics of the National Association of Social Workers. (1996). Washington, DC: Author.

Compton, B., & Galway, B. (1989). *Social work processes.* Belmont, CA: Wadsworth Publishing Co.

Cowley, A. (1993). Transpersonal social work: A theory for the 1990's. *Social Work, 38*(5), 527–34.

Cox, S., & Gallois, C. (1996). Gay and lesbian identity development: A social identity perspective. *Journal of Homosexuality, 30*(4), 1–30.

Cross, W. E. Jr. (1978). *Shades of Black: Diversity in African-American identity.* Philadelphia: Temple University Press.

Crouch, S. (1996, September 29). Race is over. *New York Times Magazine,* pp. 170–171.

Davidson, A. E. (1993). *Value development among Jewish adolescents: Processes of engagement.* Unpublished doctoral dissertation, Case Western Reserve University.

Davis, A. F. (1967). *Spearheads for reform—The social settlement and the progressive movement 1890–1914.* New York: Oxford University Press.

Devore, W., Schlesinger, E., & Devore. (1996). *Ethnic sensitive social work practice.* Boston: Allyn and Bacon.

Durkheim, E. (1951). *Suicide.* New York: Free Press.

Duska, R., & Whelan, M. (1975). *Moral development: A guide to Piaget and Kohlberg.* New York: Paulist Press.

Erikson, E. (1963). *Childhood and society.* New York: W.W. Norton Company, Inc.

Erikson, E. (1968). *Identity, youth, and crisis.* New York: W.W. Norton Company, Inc.

Erikson, E. (1980). *Identity and the life cycle.* New York: W.W. Norton Company, Inc.

Germain, C. B. (1991). *Human behavior in the social environment.* New York: Columbia University Press.

Gilligan, C. (1982). *In a different voice.* Cambridge, MA: Harvard University Press.

Gilligan, C. (1982). New maps of development: New versions of maturity. *American Journal of Orthopsychiatry, 52*(2), 199–212.

Gitterman, A. (1991). Social work practice with vulnerable populations. In A. Gitterman (Ed.), *Handbook of social work.* New York: Columbia University Press.

Gushue, G. V. (1993). Cultural identity development and family assessment: An interaction model. *Counseling Psychologist, 21*(3), 487–513.

Helms, J. E. (Ed.). (1990). *Black and white racial identity: Theory, research, and practice.* Westport, CT: Greenwood Press.

Hodge, L. H. (1917). Why a visiting teacher? In *Addresses and Proceedings of the National Education Association.* Washington DC: National Education Association.

Hoffman, P. (1994, November). The science of race. *Discover Magazine.*

Holmes, T. H., & Rahe, R. H. (1967). The social readjustment rating scale. *Journal of Psychosomatic Research, 11*(2), 214.

Hraba, J. (1994). *American ethnicity.* Itasca, IL: F. E. Peacock Publishers.

Jencks, C., et al. (1972). *Inequality: A reassessment of the effect of family and school in America.* New York: Harper and Row.

Kadushin, A. (1990). *The social work interview.* New York: Columbia University Press.

Karp, D. A., & Yoels, W. C. (1986). *Sociology and everyday life.* Itasca, IL: F. E. Peacock Publishers.

Kerwin, C., Ponterotto, J. G., Jackson, B. L., & Harris, A. (1993). Racial identity in biracial children: A qualitative investigation. *Journal of Counseling Psychology, 40*(2), 221–31.

Langston, D. (1992). Tired of playing monopoly? In M. L. Anderson & P. H. Collins (Eds.), *Race, class, and gender.* Belmont, CA: Wadsworth Publishing Co.

Levy, B. (1974). The school's role in the sex-role stereotyping of girls. In M. Wasserman (Ed.), *Demystifying school: Writings and experiences.* New York: Frederick A. Prager.

Linsay, K. (1981). *Friends as family.* Boston, MA: Beacon Press.

Loewenberg, F. M., & Dolgoff, R. (1992). *Ethical decisions for social work practice.* Itasca, IL: F. E. Peacock Publishers.

Logan, S. L. (1981). Race, identity and black children: A developmental perspective. *Social Casework, 62*(1), 47–56.

Longres, J. F. (1990). *Human behavior in the social environment.* Itasca, IL: F. E. Peacock Publishers.

Lubove, R. (1965). *The professional altruist: The emergence of social work as a career.* Cambridge, MA: Harvard University Press.

McGee, E. (1981). The transpersonal perspective: Implications for the future of personal and social development. *Social Development Issues 8*(3), 158–81.

Mead, G. H. (1934). *Mind, self, and society.* Chicago: University of Chicago Press.

Merton, R. K. (1951). *Social theory and social structure.* New York: Free Press.

Meyer, C., & Mattaini, M. (1995). *The foundations of social work practice.* Washington, DC: NASW Press.

Morrow, D. S. (1996). Coming-out issues for adult lesbians: A group intervention. *Social Work, 41*(6), 647–56.

Moses, A. E., & Hawkins, R. O. (1982). *Counseling lesbian women and gay men: A life-issues approach.* St. Louis, MO: Mosby Publishers.

National Association of Social Workers, Inc. (1996). *NASW Code of Ethics,* 7–8.

Nichols, M., & Leiblum, S. R. (1986). Lesbianism as a personal identity and social role: A model. *Affilia Journal of Women and Social Work, 1*(1), 48–59.

Ohannessian, C. M., Lerner, R. M., Lerner, J. V., & Von Eye, A. (1994). A longitudinal study of perceived family adjustment and emotional adjustment in early adolescence. *The Journal of Early Adolescence, 14*(3), 371–90.

Park, R. E. (1950). *Race and culture*. New York: Free Press.

Phinney, J. S. (1989). Stages of ethnic identity development in minority group adolescents. *Journal of Early Adolescence, 9*(1–2), 34–49.

Pinderhughes, E. (1990). *Understanding race, ethnicity, and power*. New York: Free Press.

Plummer, D. L. (1995). Patterns of racial identity development of African American adolescent males and females. *Journal of Black Psychology, 21*(2), 168–180.

Poston, W. C. (1990). The biracial identity development model: A needed addition. *Journal of Counseling and Development, 69*(2), 152–55.

Price, R. H. (1985). Work and community. *American Journal of Community Psychology, 13*(1), 1–12.

Reamer, F. (1994). *The foundations of social work knowledge*. New York: Columbia University Press.

Rhodes, M. L. (1985). Gilligan's theory of moral development as applied to social work. *Social Work, 30*(2), 101–05.

Reimer, M. S. (1983). Gender differences in moral judgment: The state of the art. *Smith College Studies in Social Work, 54*(1), 1–12.

Rothman, J. (1994). *Practice with highly vulnerable clients*. Englewood Cliffs, NJ: Prentice Hall.

Sheehy, G. (1976). *Passages*. New York: Bantam Books.

Sheehy, G. (1995). *New passages: Mapping your life across time*. New York: Ballantine Books.

Shulman, L. (1992). *The skills of helping*. Itasca, IL: F. E. Peacock Publishers.

Steer, M. (1989). A powerful concept for disability policy and service provision. *Australian Social Work, 42*(1), 43–47.

Stevens, J. W. (1997). African-American female adolescent identity development: A three dimensional perspective. *Child Welfare, 76*(1), 145–72.

Sue, D. W. (1989). Racial/cultural identity development among Asian-Americans. *AAPA Journal, 13*(1), 80–86.

Tajfel, H., Ed., & Robinson, P. (1997). *Social groups and identities: Developing the legacy of Henry Tajfel* (International Series in Social Psychology) Butterworth, Heinemann.

Tan, C. I. (1993). *The liberation of Asians*. Seattle, WA: Rational Island Publishers.

Thomas, S., & Wolfensberger, W. (1982). The importance of social imagery in interpreting societally devalued people to the public. *Rehabilitation Literature, 43*(11–12), 356–58.

Tokuno, K. A. (1986). The early adult's transition and friendships: Mechanisms of support. *Adolescence, 21*(83), 593–606.

U.S. Bureau of the Census (1987). *Statistical Abstract of the United States 1988*. Washington DC: Author.

Waterman, A. S. (1982). Identity development from adolescence to adulthood: An extension of theory and a review of research. *Developmental Psychology, 18*(3),341–58.

Weigert, A. J., & Hastings, R. (1977). Identity loss, family, and social change. *American Journal of Sociology, 82*(6), 1171–85.

Weinberg, N. (1983). Social equity and the physically disabled. *Social Work, 28*, 165–69.